On Borrowed Time?

Assessing the Threat of Mineral Depletion

D1602417

John E. Tilton

Resources for the Future
Washington, DC

Printed in the United States of America

An RFF Press book
Published by Resources for the Future
1616 P Street, NW, Washington, DC 20036–1400
www.rff.org

Library of Congress Cataloging-in-Publication Data
Tilton, John E.
  On borrowed time? : assessing the threat of mineral depletion / John E. Tilton.
       p. cm.
  Includes bibliographical references and index.
   ISBN 1-891853-58-9 (library binding : alk. paper) -- ISBN 1-891853-57-0 (pbk. : alk. paper)
   1. Geology, Economic. 2. Mines and mineral resources. I. Title.
  TN260 .T55 2002
  333.8'5--dc21
                              2002003419
                        f e d c b a

The paper in this book meets the guidelines for permanence and durability of the Committee on Production Guidelines for Book Longevity of the Council on Library Resources.

The text of this book was designed by Betsy Kulamer in Stone Serif and Stone Sans and typeset by Peter Lindeman. It was copyedited by Alfred F. Imhoff. The cover was designed by Rosenbohm Graphic Design.

About
Resources for the Future and *RFF Press*

Resources for the Future (RFF) improves environmental and natural resource policymaking worldwide through independent social science research of the highest caliber.

Founded in 1952, RFF pioneered the application of economics as a tool to develop more effective policy about the use and conservation of natural resources. Its scholars continue to employ social science methods to analyze critical issues concerning pollution control, energy policy, land and water use, hazardous waste, climate change, biodiversity, and the environmental challenges of developing countries.

RFF Press supports the mission of RFF by publishing book-length works that present a broad range of approaches to the study of natural resources and the environment. Its authors and editors include RFF staff, researchers from the larger academic and policy communities, and journalists. Audiences for RFF publications include all of the participants in the policymaking process—scholars, the media, advocacy groups, nongovernmental organizations, professionals in business and government, and the general public.

Resources for the Future

Contents

Preface

Since the early 1970s, the availability of nonrenewable mineral resources over the long run—a period spanning the coming centuries—has intrigued me. In part, this interest reflects the importance of mineral resources to human welfare. Without adequate supplies of oil, natural gas, coal, steel, aluminum, zinc, phosphate rock, and other mineral commodities, modern civilization as we know it is difficult to imagine. Many consider resource availability one of the major challenges facing humanity, along with nuclear war, population growth, and environmental preservation. Of course, these vital issues shaping the future of humankind and the rest of the world as well are not independent.

In addition, I find the topic fascinating because the debate between those who are concerned about the depletion of mineral resources, often referred to as the pessimists, and those who are unconcerned, the optimists, seems as lively and contentious today as it was three decades ago. I marvel at how this can be—how can intelligent and informed people remain so divided on such an important issue after decades of discussions and research?

Over the years, I have tried in my own way to contribute to this discussion, beginning with a short book, *The Future of Nonfuel Minerals*, which the Brookings Institution published in 1975. Other publications that I have since added to the burgeoning literature in this field are noted in the references. This study draws heavily on these earlier efforts, and in this sense is not entirely an original contribution. That, in any case, is not my objective.

Rather, I am trying to provide a concise primer on the long-run availability of mineral resources for those who are not resource economists or specialists in related fields. The goal is to offer an overview of the important issues along with the necessary conceptual tools for the reader to come to his or her own conclusions regarding the seriousness of the depletion threat and appropriate policy responses. Of course, I have my own opinions, which inevitably must creep into the presentation, though I have tried to be objective in discussing the controversial issues. The perspective is largely that of an economist, reflecting my own training and background.

An earlier version of this study served as the background paper for the Workshop on the Long-Run Availability of Mineral Commodities, which was convened by the Mining, Minerals, and Sustainable Development Project and by Resources for the Future in Washington, DC, on April 23, 2001. The pages that follow have benefited greatly from the many comments and suggestions by the 29 participants attending the workshop.

In particular, for their helpful comments and suggestions, I thank Robin G. Adams, William M. Brown, Robert D. Cairns, David Chambers, Carol A. Dahl, Joel Darmstadter, Graham A. Davis, John H. DeYoung, Jr., Peter Howie, David Humphreys, Toni Marechaux, Carmine Nappi, Raul O'Ryan, Marian Radetzki, Don Reisman, Brian J. Skinner, John Taylor, and Michael A. Toman. I also thank Thitisak Boonpramote for his research assistance, and Margaret Tilton for her editorial suggestions.

Finally, I am grateful to the Mining, Minerals, and Sustainable Development Project for an unrestricted grant, and I thank the Viola Vestal Coulter Foundation, the Kempe Foundation, and Resources for the Future for their support and encouragement as well. Of course, the usual caveat applies. The views expressed here are my own. They may or may not coincide with those of these organizations.

John E. Tilton
Golden, Colorado

Chapter 1

The Road Ahead

Mining and the consumption of nonrenewable mineral resources date back to the Bronze Age, indeed even the Stone Age. So for millennia, they have made the lives of people nicer, easier, and more secure.

What is new is the pace of exploitation. Humankind has consumed more aluminum, copper, iron and steel, phosphate rock, diamonds, sulfur, coal, oil, natural gas, and even sand and gravel during the past century than all earlier centuries together. Moreover, the pace continues to accelerate, so that today the world annually produces and consumes nearly all mineral commodities at record rates (see Box 1-1).

At least four underlying forces are driving this explosion in use. First, advances in technology allow the extraction of copper, coal, and many other mineral commodities at lower and lower costs. This pushes prices down and consumption up. Second, advances in technology also permit new and better mineral commodities serving a range of new needs. For example, the development of tinplate (steel sheet coated with a thin layer of tin) led to the widespread use of metal cans to preserve food and beverages. Third, rapidly rising living standards in many parts of the globe are increasing the demand across the board for goods and services, including many that use mineral commodities intensively in their production. Fourth, the surge in world population means more and more people with needs to satisfy. Of these forces, only population growth shows any sign of abating.

The sharp rise in mineral consumption and production has, understandably, raised concerns about the long-run availability of mineral commodities. Because mineral resources are by nature nonrenewable, their supply is limited.

Box 1-1. Nature of Mineral Commodities

It is common to distinguish between three types or classes of mineral commodities—fuels, metals, and nonmetals. Fuels include oil, natural gas, coal, and uranium, and are valued for the energy they can produce. Metals are employed primarily as materials. Iron and steel, aluminum, and copper are the most important metals, but there are many others as well. Nonmetals are used primarily for construction, other industrial applications, and fertilizer production. They include sand and gravel, stone, limestone, sulfur, phosphate rock, and numerous other substances.

Although all mineral commodities are produced from mineral resources, they differ greatly even within the same class. Oil and natural gas, for example, are pumped from wells, whereas coal and uranium are mined like many metal commodities. Magnesium, however, is extracted from seawater. The production of sand and gravel is relatively uncomplicated, whereas the processing of copper and steel requires highly sophisticated technologies. Molybdenum is recovered primarily as a by-product of copper mining, and lead is largely supplied by the recycling of old scrap. Cobalt is produced in only a few countries and is widely traded. Sand and gravel, however, are widely available and expensive to ship, and so they enter international trade on only a modest scale.

The earth contains only so much oil, copper, and other mineral commodities. Demand, conversely, continues year after year. As a result, many believe that it is just a matter of time before the availability of mineral supplies is threatened. Should the rate of mineral exploitation continue to grow as it has during the past several decades, it is argued, mineral depletion will create serious problems sooner rather than later. Moreover, as society is forced to exploit lower grade and more remote deposits, the environmental and other social costs associated with producing and using mineral commodities are likely to rise, perhaps limiting their use even before depletion.

Concern about the long-run availability of mineral resources, however, is not universal. On the other side of the debate are those who believe that the market coupled with appropriate public policies is sufficiently robust to deal with any threats. Pending shortages push mineral prices up, which in turn unleashes a host of countervailing forces. Exploration rises, increasing the likelihood of new discoveries. Research and development produces new technologies that allow the production of mineral commodities from previously unusable resources. Recycling increases. Less scarce, and possibly renewable, resources are substituted for minerals facing growing shortages. Higher prices also reduce the use of mineral commodities, both because consumers can afford less and because they shift the mix of goods and services they purchase, reducing those items whose prices have risen.

The stakes are not trivial. Nonrenewable resources matter. Long-run availability has consequences for the world's ability to sustain its current population, let alone accommodate increases. Similarly, it has consequences for sustaining our modern civilization. Without nonrenewable resources, there would be no telephones, televisions, or computers. No automobiles, bicycles, trucks, buses, tractors, ships, or airplanes. No electricity. High-rise buildings and large cities could not exist. Modern medicine and science would be unknown. For many thousands of years humanity survived without the use of nonrenewable resources beyond stones and rocks, but at what quality of existence?

As Chapter 2 will show, the debate over resource availability is not new. It can be traced back at least 200 years to the Classical economists, though the past 30 years have been particularly active. Much of the recent literature, however, is technical, written by economists, geologists, ecologists, and other specialists in a manner that the interested layperson often finds difficult to follow.

Purpose and Scope

This study proposes to provide a framework for analyzing the ongoing debate over mineral resource availability, and to review the important literature in a manner that the nonspecialist can appreciate. It attempts to answer a number of questions: What have we learned? On what do the experts now agree? Where do they continue to disagree, and why? What are the important implications of what has been learned? In particular, is modern civilization—like a sailor adrift at sea in a lifeboat with only a few days of water and food left on board—living on borrowed time, as it runs through the vital mineral resources on which its very survival depends?

The focus is on the availability of mineral commodities over the coming decades and centuries, or what is often called the mineral-depletion or mineral-exhaustion problem. I do not address availability problems that arise for reasons other than mineral depletion. Strikes, cartels, price controls and other government policies, monopolies, adverse weather, accidents, booms in the business cycle, and even insufficient investment in exploration and mineral development can all for a time cause shortages of mineral commodities. Such shortages in almost all cases are temporary, lasting from a few days to perhaps a decade. Though they can cause considerable dislocation and hardship while they last, they fall outside the scope of this inquiry.

Terminology

Availability, scarcity, and shortages are terms frequently encountered in this study. As Chapter 3 will discuss, there are many measures and definitions of mineral resource availability, all of which have their limitations. For my purpose, however, it is important that trends in availability reflect the extent to which mineral depletion is a growing threat to the long-run welfare of society. For this reason, I measure availability by what has to be given up in terms of other goods and services to obtain a mineral commodity. Economists refer to this sacrifice as the *opportunity cost*. So if the availability of oil is declining, this implies that over time more of other goods and services must be forgone to obtain an additional barrel, and in turn that the threat of depletion is growing.

The term *shortage* is often used to reflect an excess of demand over supply at the prevailing market price for a particular commodity, such as copper. Such situations can occur if governments or companies control prices. They are, however, unusual, because normally when demand exceeds supply price rises, bringing the two back into balance.

In any case, this definition is too narrow for our purposes. If rising prices are needed to keep supply equal to demand, consumers are likely to find the commodity more and more difficult to afford. For them, it is in shorter and shorter supply and scarce. For this reason, we define the terms shortage and scarcity more broadly. A growing shortage or increasing scarcity is simply the same as declining availability, and may occur even though demand and supply remain in balance thanks to rising prices.

We also need to distinguish between mineral resources and mineral commodities, and between renewable and nonrenewable resources. *Mineral commodities*, such as copper, are produced from mineral resources, such as chalcopyrite and other copper-containing minerals. *Mineral resources* are the legacy of geologic processes that take place over geologic time, measured not in decades and centuries, but in hundreds of millions of years. Because the time required for their formation is so vast from the perspective of any meaningful time scale for people, mineral resources are considered *nonrenewable*. In contrast, many other resources, such as water, air, forests, fish, and solar energy, are considered *renewable*. Fish caught in the sea and trees cut in the forest can be replaced within a much shorter period of time. So their current use need not result in less being available in the future. Just how significant the difference is between nonrenewable and renewable resources, however, is debatable, because renewable resources, like nonrenewable resources, can suffer from depletion if overexploited. We will revisit this issue in Chapter 7.

Organization of the Book

The presentation following this introduction proceeds in the following way. Chapter 2 examines the historical evolution of concerns over the long-run availability of mineral resources. It reviews the pioneering works of Thomas Malthus, David Ricardo, and Harold Hotelling, as well as the much more abundant literature since the 1970s.

Chapter 3 identifies different measures used to assess long-run trends in resource availability, and examines their strengths and weaknesses. It considers physical measures, such as reserves and the resource base, as well as purely economic measures, such as costs and prices. It explores the concepts of user costs, economic and physical depletion, as well as Ricardian and Hotelling rents. It raises the possibility that mineral commodities may become more, rather than less, available over time.

Chapter 4, using measures described in Chapter 3, examines trends in resource scarcity during the past century. It covers the seminal work of Harold Barnett and Chandler Morse on production costs, along with the more recent work of Margaret Slade and others on mineral commodity prices. It finds that mineral resources, despite their widespread and accelerating use, have not become more scarce during the past century.

Chapter 5—acknowledging that past trends are not necessarily a good guide to the future—looks at the availability of mineral commodities in the near term (the next 50 years) and the more distant future. It examines the work of Brian Skinner on the geologic nature of mineral deposit formation, and its implications for future scarcity. It also introduces the cumulative supply curve, a conceptual technique for categorizing the various factors shaping future trends in mineral resource availability. The chapter finds that the distant future with respect to mineral resource availability is at this time unknown, which helps explain why the debate over this issue continues. But it also suggests that society, if it wishes and is willing to cover the costs, can obtain considerable information on the prospects for future shortages by carrying out more research on the nature and incidence of subeconomic mineral deposits.

Chapter 6 turns to the environmental and other social costs associated with mineral exploitation, and assesses the threat they pose to the long-run availability of mineral commodities. It examines the ability of public policy to force mineral-producing firms to pay their full costs of production, particularly in light of the difficulties of measuring social costs and of regulating small-scale artisanal mining. It also assesses the ability of mineral-producing companies to reduce costs—assuming that all social costs are internalized—by new technology and other means. The chapter ends by suggesting that economists and other social scientists are likely to play an increasing role in society's efforts to keep the adverse effects of mineral depletion at bay, complementing the important contributions that engineers and physical scientists have traditionally made.

Chapter 7, the final chapter, highlights the findings, and explores their implications for sustainable development; for green accounting; for the protection of indigenous cultures and other social goods; for conservation, recycled materials, and renewable resources; and for global population. Among other things, this chapter suggests that the link between mineral resource availability and sustainable development is much looser than many presume. Declining resource availability need not prevent sustainable development, just as growing resource availability does not ensure it.

An appendix by Peter Howie and a glossary follow chapter 7. The appendix shows the trends in the real prices since 1870 for petroleum, natural gas, coal, iron ore, copper, and a few other important mineral commodities. The glossary briefly defines many of the more technical terms used in this book.

In addition, in many chapters supplemental information is found in boxes separated from the main text. This material provides specific examples of the points being raised, describes important concepts that may not be familiar to some readers, and in other ways adds to the analysis in the main text. Notes and references are at the ends of the chapters.

Chapter 2

Evolving Concerns

Resource shortages, and presumably concerns over resource availability, can be traced far back in time. Some 3,000 years ago, for example, the Philistines, Dorians, and others invaded the eastern Mediterranean area. For nearly a century, they severed the trading routes that Greece had relied upon for the tin it needed to make bronze. According to Maurice and Smithson (1984), the resulting shortages encouraged the Greeks to develop the means to produce iron, and thus contributed to the end of the Bronze Age and the beginning of the Iron Age in Europe.

Other examples can be found of early concerns over resource availability. For our purposes, however, it is sufficient to start with the classical economists writing at the end of the eighteenth century and the beginning of the nineteenth century.

Classical Economists, 1798–1880

Among the classical economists, Thomas Malthus is the best known for his views on resource availability and the human condition. His first published work, *An Essay on the Principle of Population*, appeared anonymously in 1798 and was republished under his name in five subsequent editions during his lifetime. In this influential treatise, he argues that population left unchecked tends to grow continuously while tillable land is limited. As more and more labor works the available land, output per worker falls until it reaches that level just sufficient to sustain life. At this point, misery or vice prevents further population growth. In his second edition, Malthus introduces the possibility that "prudential constraint" might limit population growth before living standards fall to the subsistence level. Despite this important qualification, the public generally associates Malthus with a very pessimistic view of the prospects for human welfare. Indeed, thanks in part to his writings, economics over the years has often been called the "dismal science."

David Ricardo extends Malthus's analysis in his *Principles of Political Economy and Taxation*, first published in 1817. Most important, he takes into account quality differences in agricultural land. He assumes the best or most fertile land is worked first. As population increases and the demand for food rises, more land of poorer and poorer quality is brought into production. As food prices increase to cover the higher costs of farming the marginal fields, the owners of the more fertile lands earn a surplus, commonly referred to as *economic rent* or *Ricardian rent*.[1] Output per worker also falls as in Malthus's world. However, the reason for the decline is the inferior quality of the new lands brought into production, rather than the addition of more workers to a given amount of (similar quality) land.

Whereas Malthus ignores mining and nonrenewable resources, Ricardo points out that mineral deposits vary in quality, just like land. As a result, he claims, his analysis of land is equally applicable to minerals. He also recognizes that it is possible to discover new mineral deposits and to develop new mining technology. It is interesting, though, that he does not consider the depletable nature of mines, and thus fails to focus on what many consider to be the fundamental difference between nonrenewable and renewable resources.

In certain ways, Ricardo is both more and less pessimistic than Malthus. Declining resource availability in his analysis causes labor productivity to fall, which occurs either immediately or at the time that poorer-quality land is first brought into production. With Malthus, problems arise only after all the available agriculture land is in use. Conversely, in Ricardo's world it is always possible to bring more land into production, as long as declining fertility is tolerated.

John Stuart Mill, the last of the classical economists we consider, develops the views of both Malthus and Ricardo in his *Principles of Political Economy*, which first appeared in 1848. Mill argues that Ricardian scarcity, arising from the need to exploit land of poorer fertility, will likely occur long before all the land available for agriculture is brought into production. Indeed, he contends that the land available for agriculture is far more extensive than Malthus presumes. He also argues that the adverse effects of uncontrolled population growth may very well encourage people to limit their offspring before living standards are driven down to subsistence. He recognizes as well that new technology can offset the tendency for resource scarcity to reduce living standards. For these reasons, his view of the human condition is more optimistic than those of Malthus and Ricardo.

The Conservation Movement, 1890–1920

The next interesting wave of concern over resource availability surfaced toward the end of the nineteenth century in the conservation movement. Industrialization coupled with the closing of the U.S. frontier and the rapid exploitation of once vast tracks of virgin forests fostered this development, which was largely a political and social movement.[2] Unlike Malthus, Ricardo, and Mill, the leaders of the conservation movement were not economists. Some, such as Theodore Roosevelt and Gifford Pinchot, were public figures. Many others were natural scientists.

As a result, the considerable literature associated with the conservation movement displays no coherent economic core. A reduction in physical supply is directly equated with a decline in resource availability, as the following frequently cited excerpt from *The Fight for Conservation* (Pinchot 1910, 123–124) so nicely illustrates:

> The five indispensably essential materials in our civilization are wood, water, coal, iron, and agricultural products. . . . We have timber for less than thirty years at the present rate of cutting. The figures indicate that our demands upon the forest have increased twice as fast as our population. We have anthracite coal for but fifty years, and bituminous coal for less than two hundred. Our supplies of iron ore, mineral oil, and natural gas are being rapidly depleted, and many of the great fields are already exhausted. Mineral resources such as these when once gone are gone forever.

The conservation movement also viewed natural resources and nature as more multidimensional, with the various components more interdependent, and the whole far more complex, than the classical economists. So our critical dependence on nature is not just economic, but also psychological and even spiritual. Nature in its wonder promotes human values. Conservation is the prudent use of resources, which goes far beyond the economist's concept of efficiency. It entails using, if possible, renewable resources in place of nonrenewable resources, more abundant nonrenewable resources in place of less abundant nonrenewable resources, and recycled products in place of primary resources. Many of these ideas continue to flourish in the writings of present-day ecologists.

Whereas the conservation movement was largely concentrated in North America during the 1890–1920 period, similar concerns emerged in other industrializing countries and at other times. W. Stanley Jevons (1865), for example, warned the United Kingdom that its limited coal resources threatened its future industrial growth.

World War II and the Early Postwar Period, 1940–1965

During the 1930s, the world was largely preoccupied with the Great Depression. Toward the end of this decade and throughout the first half of the 1940s, concerns over resource availability returned, but they focused on the short-run issue of securing adequate supplies for the war effort. Shortly after the war, however, the long-run availability of mineral resources once again rose to prominence as the world examined the implications of first reconstruction and then long-run economic development. In the United States, these concerns led to the creation of the President's Material Policy Commission, more popularly known as the Paley Commission after its chair, William S. Paley. The commission, which published its hefty five-volume report in 1952, assessed the adequacy of the world's mineral resources to meet future needs. In the words of Volume 1:

> The nature of the problem can perhaps be successfully over-simplified by saying that the consumption of almost all materials is expanding at compound rates and is thus pressing harder and harder against resources which, whatever else they may be doing, are not similarly expanding. This Materials Problem is thus not the sort of "shortage" problem, local and transient, which in the past has found its solution in price changes which have brought supply and demand back into balance. The terms of the Materials Problem we face today are larger and more pervasive. (President's Materials Policy Commission 1952, 2)

The Paley Commission report encouraged the Ford Foundation in 1952 to provide the funding needed to establish Resources for the Future, a nonprofit corporation for research and education in the development, conservation, and use of natural resources. During the next several decades, Resources for the Future sponsored a number of studies on the long-run availability of mineral resources, including the influential study by Barnett and Morse (1963), one of two seminal works that shaped the debate over the long-run availability of mineral resources during the latter half of the twentieth century.[3] The second, discussed at the end of this chapter, is the article by Harold Hotelling (1931), "The Economics of Exhaustible Resources."

Barnett and Morse draw a sharp distinction between the physical availability of resources and economic scarcity. During the latter half of the nineteenth century, for example, the actual and potential supply of whale oil declined as many species of whales were hunted almost to extinction. The development of low-cost petroleum products and electricity, however, filled the needs previously satisfied by whale oil, and so prevented this physical decline from producing economic scarcity.

Using measures of economic scarcity, Barnett and Morse find that both renewable and nonrenewable resources—but in particular nonrenewable mineral resources—became more, not less, available between 1870 and 1957 (the period they examined), despite the explosion in resource use during the twentieth century. They attribute this favorable outcome largely to the ability of technological change to offset the adverse effects of resource depletion. This surprising finding, which stood in stark contrast to the perceived wisdom of the day, stimulated a research boom in this area.[4] In Chapter 4, we will return to the Barnett and Morse study and the subsequent literature it spawned.

Limits to Growth and Social Costs, 1970–2000

In investing, it is often said, timing is everything. The same may hold, at least on occasion, for academic publications. In 1972, Donella H. Meadows and her colleagues published their book *The Limits to Growth*. Using an analytical technique called *system dynamics*, they construct a model that generates scenarios of future worlds. In their base-case scenario, the one that they believe most likely to evolve barring corrective public policies, they foresee the collapse of per capita food and industrial output as a result of mineral resource exhaustion by the middle of the twenty-first century. Although economists and others severely criticized the study for its measures of resource availability (as Chapter 3 will explain) and other shortcomings, it nevertheless was widely read and very influential, thanks in large part to its timing.

Shortly after the book appeared, the Middle Eastern nations belonging to the Organization of the Petroleum Exporting Countries (OPEC) imposed an embargo on oil exports to the United States and the Netherlands for their support of Israel during the 1973 Middle Eastern war. Simultaneously, OPEC as a whole engineered a threefold increase in the world price of oil by withholding exports. Prices for many other mineral commodities also rose sharply in tandem with an economic boom in Japan, North America, and Western Europe.

Of course, temporary shortages caused by embargoes, cartels, and economic booms do not necessarily mean that depletion is a problem. Still, the dislocations, though temporary, were painful, aggravated in part by market controls in some consuming countries that prevented commodity prices from rising to their market-clearing levels. These problems focused public attention on resource availability in general and on *The Limits to Growth* in particular. Many saw the disruptions of the early 1970s as a first warning that depletion was in the offing—along with more permanent and serious shortages.

The widely expected scarcity, however, failed to occur during the 1980s and 1990s as the price of oil, coal, natural gas, iron ore, aluminum, copper, and many other mineral commodities actually declined, suggesting growing rather than declining resource availability. As a result, fears of resource depletion, though not evaporating completely, did subside. They were replaced by growing concerns over environmental pollution and other social costs, such as the losses of biodiversity, indigenous cultures, and pristine wilderness associated with mineral extraction, processing, and use. The following quotations reflect this shift in concern:[5]

> The difference between the emerging breed of environmentalists ("spacemen") and the older breed of neo-Malthusians is that the latter mostly failed to see that the environment itself is a limited resource. Neo-Malthusians mainly emphasized potential scarcities of resources. . . . There are many, including myself, who believe that given a reasonably free market, technology can generally be depended upon to find a substitute for almost any scarce material resource input (except energy itself). However, there are no plausible technological substitutes for climatic stability, stratospheric ozone, air, water, topsoil, vegetation—especially forests—or species diversity. In every case, total loss would be catastrophic to the human race, and probably lethal. Although technology can create (and money can buy) many things, it cannot create a substitute for the atmosphere or the biosphere. Technological optimism, in this regard, is simply misguided. (Ayres 1993, 195)
>
> At the end of the twentieth century, we are faced with two closely related threats. First, there is the increasing rate at which we are consuming mineral resources, the basic materials on which civilization depends. Although we have not yet experienced global mineral shortages, they are on the horizon. Second, there is the growing pollution caused by the extraction and consumption of mineral resources, which threatens to make earth's surface uninhabitable. We may well ponder which of these will first limit the continued improvement of our standard of living. (Kesler 1994, iii)

Another interesting example of this shift is *Beyond the Limits* (Meadows and others 1992), a sequel to *The Limits to Growth*, written for the twentieth anniversary of the latter's publication. Like the original volume, *Beyond the Limits* uses a system dynamics model to generate scenarios of the future. The base-case scenario in both studies sees modern civilization collapsing during the twenty-first century. In *Beyond the Limits*, however, environmental damage arising from the production and use of resources, rather than resource exhaustion, causes the collapse.

Hotelling and the Theory of Exhaustible Resources

Although the preceding discussion brings us up to the present, it omits an important development that Harold Hotelling (1931) fathered with his article,

"The Economics of Exhaustible Resources." In this piece (which we examine at the end of this survey because of its importance and its complexity), Hotelling explores the optimal output over time for a mine with a given amount of known resources. To simplify the problem, he makes six strong assumptions: (1) The mine's goal or objective is to maximize the present value (see Box 2-1) of its current and future profits. (2) The mine is perfectly competitive and so has no control over the price it receives for its output. (3) There is no uncertainty, so the mine knows the size and nature of its resource stock as well as current and future costs and prices. (4) The mine's output is not limited by existing capacity or other constraints, allowing the mine to produce as little as nothing and as much as its entire remaining resource stock during any particular time period. (5) The mine's resource stock is homogeneous, so grade and other qualities do not vary. (6) There is no technological change.

Under these conditions, Hotelling shows that firms exploiting an exhaustible resource stock behave differently than firms in other industries where all inputs are unconstrained over the long run. The latter, following the principles of any introductory economics textbook, maximize the present value of their profits by continuing each period to expand their output up to the point where the extra or marginal cost of producing one more unit just equals the prevailing market price. At this point, any further expansion of output will not increase profits and may reduce them as the cost of producing more equals or exceeds the additional revenue that the firms earn.

Box 2-1. Present Value

A dollar received today is worth more than a dollar received one year or ten years in the future, for the dollar received today can be invested and earn a rate of return, or interest, during the coming year or decade. Studies in economics and finance use the concept of *present value* to determine the worth today of revenues that will be received or expenses that will be incurred in the future. This concept takes the future revenue or expenditure and discounts it for the time value of money to determine its present value. If, for example, the time value of money (approximated by the interest one can earn on a riskless investment) is 5 percent a year, then the present value of a dollar of profit one year from now is 95 cents (or a dollar divided by 1.05). And the present value of a dollar of profit five years from now is 78 cents (or a dollar divided by 1.05^5). In this way, one can take a stream of net revenues (revenues minus expenditures) during the coming years and calculate its present value.

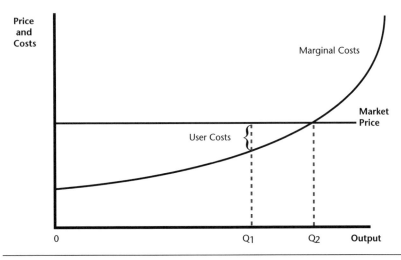

Figure 2-1. Market Price and Optimal Output for a Mineral Commodity Producer

Resource firms, conversely, have to take into account that each unit of output today means less profit in the future. In a world where ore is homogeneous (as Hotelling assumes), increasing output by one unit today results in a reduction of output by one unit in the final period of operation and the loss of the profits associated with that unit. In a world where the ore is heterogeneous (i.e., where some ores are cheaper to mine and process than others), an increase in output today means that the future must exploit poorer-quality resources, causing higher costs and lower profits.

So in addition to the costs of producing an additional unit, there are opportunity costs, commonly referred to as *user costs*, which equal the present value of the lost future profits. As a result, a resource firm has an incentive to expand its output during any particular period only up to the point at which the additional or marginal costs of producing one more unit plus user costs equal the market price. Figure 2-1 illustrates this difference. The firm with a fixed resource stock produces at Q_1. The firm without fixed inputs expands its output to Q_2.

Because user costs are the present value of the lost future profits associated with a unit increase in current production, they also reflect the present value of the extra future profits a firm would realize from having the additional resources needed to produce one more unit of output. This means that user costs measure the current value of an additional unit of mineral resource in the ground. Moreover, in the world of Hotelling, where the mineral resource stock is homogenous, user costs multiplied by the available mineral resource give the current value of the total stock of the mineral resource in the ground.

Hotelling also points out that mineral resources in the ground are assets, and so they must under his assumptions earn a rate of return (r) comparable to other types of assets with similar risks. If this were not the case—if the rate of return on mineral resources were lower than that of other comparable assets—it would pay their owners to extract and sell these assets as soon as possible and to invest the resulting profits in other assets whose returns were higher. This behavior, which would drive down mineral prices in the current period and raise them in later periods (when less would be available), would continue until the rate of return from holding mineral resources in the ground just equaled the rate of return on other comparable assets. Conversely, if the rate of return on mineral resources were higher than that of other comparable assets, the owners of mineral resources would be reluctant to exploit them. This would drive current prices up and future prices down, and in the process cause the rate of return earned by holding mineral resources to decline until it reached that of other assets.

This theoretical finding has important implications for mineral availability. Specifically, it anticipates that mineral resources in the ground should become less available as their value or price rises exponentially over time at the rate of r percent, where r is the rate of return on other comparable market assets.

For several decades, Hotelling's article attracted little attention. Since the 1960s, however, some of the best minds in the field of economics have focused on this topic, attracted in part by the challenge of solving complex intertemporal optimization problems with new developments in advanced mathematics. The resulting literature (reviewed in Peterson and Fisher 1977, Bohi and Toman 1984, Krautkraemer 1998, and Neumayer 2000) relaxes many of Hotelling's assumptions. It also extends the scope from the optimal behavior for an individual mine to the optimal behavior for society as a whole in light of the finite nature of resources. These more recent works take into account a host of factors: exploration and the discovery of new mineral deposits, technological change from exploration to the reuse of mineral commodities, ore bodies with different grades and qualities, uncertainty and imperfect knowledge, recycling, market power that allows firms some control over price, and firm objectives other than maximizing the present value of current and future profits.

It is not surprising that relaxing Hotelling's assumptions alters his findings. No longer does the value of mineral resources in the ground have to rise at r percent over time. Indeed, with exploration and new technology, the value of mineral resources in the ground may even fall, implying that resource availability is increasing. Nevertheless, Hotelling's article and the subsequent work it stimulated play an important role in our understanding of the long-run availability of mineral resources. In particular, we will return to Hotelling and other works on the theory of exhaustible resources in the next two chapters.

Notes

1. It is helpful to think of Ricardian rent as the amount a tenant farmer would pay a landlord for the use of his land. The greater the fertility of the land, the more the tenant would be willing to pay and the more the landlord would demand.

2. This section is largely based on the interesting chapter (Chapter 4) on the conservation movement found in Barnett and Morse 1963, which in turn draws from Hays 1959.

3. A sample of other studies on resource availability that Resources for the Future has sponsored over the years includes Adelman 1973; Bohi and Toman 1984; Darmstadter and others 1977; Herfindahl 1959; Kneese and others 1970; Landsberg and Schurr 1968; Landsberg and others 1963; Manners 1971; Manthy 1978; Potter and Christy 1962; and Smith 1979.

4. Chapter 2 of Barnett and Morse 1963, entitled "Contemporary Views on Social Aspects of Resources," contains an interesting survey of the views of government and various disciplines (naturalism, ecology, demography, political science, and economics) prevailing at the time this book was written.

5. Earlier writers anticipated the concern over the environmental constraint on resource exploitation of the 1990s (e.g., Brooks and Andrews 1974).

References

Adelman, M.A. 1973. *The World Petroleum Market.* Baltimore, MD: Johns Hopkins University Press for Resources for the Future.

Ayres, R.U. 1993. Cowboys, Cornucopians and Long-Run Sustainability. *Ecological Economics* 8: 189–207.

Barnett, H.J., and C. Morse. 1963. *Scarcity and Growth.* Baltimore, MD: Johns Hopkins University Press for Resources for the Future.

Bohi, D.R., and M.A. Toman. 1984. *Analyzing Nonrenewable Resource Supply.* Baltimore, MD: Johns Hopkins University Press for Resources for the Future.

Brooks, D.B., and P.W. Andrews. 1984. Mineral Resources, Economic Growth, and World Population. *Science* 185: 13–19.

Darmstadter, J. and others. 1977. *How Industrial Societies Use Energy: A Comparative Analysis.* Baltimore, MD: Johns Hopkins University Press for Resources for the Future.

Fisher, A.C. 1979. Measures of Natural Resource Scarcity. In *Scarcity and Growth Reconsidered*, edited by V. K. Smith. Baltimore, MD: Johns Hopkins University Press for Resources for the Future, 249–275.

Hays, S.P. 1959. *Conservation and the Gospel of Efficiency: The Progressive Conservation Movement, 1890–1920.* Cambridge, MA: Harvard University Press.

Herfindahl, O.C. 1959. *Copper Costs and Prices: 1870–1957.* Baltimore, MD: Johns Hopkins University Press for Resources for the Future.

Hotelling, H. 1931. The Economics of Exhaustible Resources. *Journal of Political Economy* 392: 137–175.

Jevons, W.S. 1865. *The Coal Question.* London: Macmillan.

Kesler, S.E. 1994. *Mineral Resources, Economics and the Environment.* New York: Macmillan.

Kneese, A.V. 1970. *Economics and the Environment: A Materials Balance Approach*. Baltimore, MD: Johns Hopkins University Press for Resources for the Future.

Krautkraemer, J.A. 1998. Nonrenewable Resource Scarcity. *Journal of Economic Literature* 36: 2065–2107.

Landsberg, H.H., and S.H. Schurr. 1968. *Energy in the United States: Sources, Uses, and Policy Issues*. Baltimore, MD: Johns Hopkins University Press for Resources for the Future.

Landsberg, H.H., and others. 1963. *Resources in America's Future: Patterns of Requirements and Availabilities, 1960-2000*. Baltimore, MD: Johns Hopkins University Press for Resources for the Future

Manners, G. 1971. *The Changing World Market for Iron Ore, 1950–1980*. Baltimore, MD: Johns Hopkins University Press for Resources for the Future.

Manthey, R.S. 1978. *Natural Resource Commodities—A Century of Statistics*. Baltimore, MD: Johns Hopkins University Press for Resources for the Future.

Maurice, C., and C. W. Smithson. 1984. *The Doomsday Myth: 10,000 Years of Economic Crises*. Stanford, CA: Hoover Institution Press.

Meadows, D. H., and others. 1972. *The Limits to Growth*. New York: Universe Books.

Meadows, D. H., and others. 1992. *Beyond the Limits*. Post Mills, VT: Chelsea Green Publishing.

Neumayer, E. 2000. Scarce or Abundant? The Economics of Natural Resource Availability. *Journal of Economic Surveys* 143: 307–335.

Peterson, F.M., and A.C. Fisher. 1977. The Exploitation of Extractive Resources: A Survey. *Economic Journal* 87: 681–721.

Pinchot, G. 1910. *The Fight for Conservation*. New York: Doubleday, Page and Company.

Potter, N., and F. T. Christy, Jr. 1962. *Trends in Natural Resource Commodities: Statistics of Prices, Output, Consumption, Foreign Trade, and Employment in the United States*. Baltimore, MD: Johns Hopkins University Press for Resources for the Future.

President's Materials Policy Commission. 1952. *Resources for Freedom, Volume I—Foundations for Growth and Security*. Washington, DC: U.S. Government Printing Office.

Smith, V.K. 1979. *Scarcity and Growth Reconsidered*. Baltimore, MD: Johns Hopkins University Press for Resources for the Future

Chapter 3

Imperfect Measures

There are many ways to measure resource availability. Although none are perfect, some are better than others. This chapter first considers measures that are entirely or largely physical in nature. These measures are frequently encountered in the literature and have considerable intuitive appeal. It then reviews measures that are economic in nature. Although all the economic measures have shortcomings, we will see that they are more useful than physical measures for assessing the long-run threat from mineral depletion. In Chapter 4, as a result, we will rely on economic measures to identify the historical trends in mineral commodity availability.

Physical Measures

The logic behind physical measures is both simple and appealing. As Chapter 1 noted, because the earth is finite, it contains a fixed amount of oil, coal, iron, copper, and any other particular substance. Consequently, the supply of all mineral commodities is a fixed stock. Physical measures attempt to assess the remaining stock at any point. The demand for mineral commodities, conversely, is a flow variable that continues year after year. Thus eventually demand must consume the available supply, causing the physical exhaustion of the commodity. To assess how long the available stock will last—the life expectancy of the commodity—one has only to forecast trends in its future use.

This view of the depletion process, in large part because it is so logical, is frequently encountered. Over the years, as we saw in Chapter 2, it has greatly influenced the literature, from Malthus to the Conservation Movement to more recent concerns over limits to growth. Although Hotelling only assumes an individual mine has a fixed stock of mineral resources, many of his followers have extended this assumption to the world as a whole.

Reserves

Though the logic behind physical measures is simple, estimating the remaining available stock of a mineral commodity raises some difficult issues. The most common approach is to use reserves or measures closely related to reserves. By definition, reserves are the quantities of a mineral commodity, such as oil or copper, found in subsurface resources (fields, deposits) that are both known and profitable to exploit with existing technology and prices.

Data on reserves for individual countries and the world as a whole are readily available from the U.S. Geological Survey, from similar government agencies in other countries, and from international organizations. The second column of Table 3-1 shows the world reserves in 1999 for a sample of mineral commodities. By themselves, they are not particularly enlightening. Normally, one uses such data to calculate mineral commodity life expectancies. This requires forecasts of future demand, along with estimates of how much of the future production will come from primary production and mining, and how much will come from secondary production and recycling (see Box 3-1). It is only primary production, of course, that depletes reserves.

Table 3-1 deals with this issue by showing life expectancies assuming primary production will grow at annual rates of 0, 2, and 5 percent. The average rate of growth in primary production during the past 25 years for each mineral commodity is also shown in Table 3-1. In most cases, this average growth rate falls between 0 and 4 percent. Lead and tin are the exceptions. Their growth has averaged a negative 0.5 percent annually.

It is not surprising that life expectancies vary greatly. The faster future demand and primary production are expected to grow, the lower life expectancies are, often by many years. For a few mineral commodities, such as magnesium (recovered from seawater) and potash, which are not shown in Table 3-1, reserves are sufficient to last for millennia at current rates of production. For most, however, the results are more troubling, suggesting that many mineral commodities will be gone within a century, and even within a few decades in the case of oil, copper, lead, nickel, silver, tin, and zinc.

This pessimistic scenario, however, presumes that reserves reflect the fixed stock of mineral commodities remaining to be exploited. This simply is not so. Reserves indicate the amount of a mineral commodity found in deposits that are known and profitable to extract with current technology and prices. Although extraction over time is depleting reserves, both the discovery of new

---

Box 3-1. Primary and Secondary Production

The supply of mineral commodities comes from both primary production and secondary production. Primary production entails the extraction and processing of mineral resources from subsurface deposits. Mineral commodities can be recovered as separate or individual products (usually the case for oil, coal, bauxite, iron, sand and gravel, and phosphate rock), or as joint products (often the case for gold, silver, lead, zinc, copper, molybdenum). Depending on their importance to the economic viability of the mine, joint products can be main products, coproducts, or by-products.

Secondary production augments the supply of many mineral commodities by recycling new and old scrap. New scrap arises in the process of manufacturing products, such as the stamping of fenders for new automobiles. Old scrap is material found in consumer and producers goods, such as old automobiles, that have come to the end of their useful lives. Only a portion of the scrap generated by society is recycled. This is because primary production is cheaper than recycling some sources of scrap, not because the mineral commodity contained in the scrap has been destroyed. The lead once used as an additive in gasoline and paint, for example, still exists, and indeed may even pose a serious environmental problem, but it is not recycled because it is far less expensive to acquire new supplies of lead from primary production.

---

deposits by exploration and also the conversion of known but uneconomic resources into profitable deposits by new technology add to reserves. Indeed, even in a static world with no exploration or new technology, reserves can increase as a result of rising mineral commodity prices or declining costs of labor, capital, and the other factors of production employed by the mineral industries.

Because exploration, new technology, and the other factors do increase reserves over time, reserves should not be thought of as long-run indicators of mineral availability, but rather as working inventories that energy and mineral companies can increase by investing in exploration and new technology. In many mineral industries, once reserves reach 20 to 30 years of current production, companies have little incentive to invest in further developing their reserves. The expense of finding new reserves that will not be needed for two or three decades is simply not worth incurring at this time.

Some studies attempt to overcome the inherent problems of using reserves to measure mineral availability by increasing reserves in an arbitrary manner. *The Limits to Growth* (Meadows and others 1972), for example, takes recent fig-

Table 3-1. Life Expectancies of World Reserves, Selected Mineral Commodities

Mineral Commodity[a]	1999 Reserves[b]	1997–1999 Average Annual Primary Production[b]	Life Expectancy in Years, at Three Growth Rates in Primary Production[c]			Average Annual Growth in Production, 1975–1999 (percent)
			0%	2%	5%	
Coal	9.9×10^{11}	4.6×10^9	216	84	49	1.1
Crude oil	1.0×10^{12}	2.4×10^{10}	44	31	23	0.8
Natural gas	5.1×10^{15}	8.1×10^{13}	64	41	29	2.9
Aluminum	2.5×10^{10}	1.2×10^8	202	81	48	2.9
Copper	3.4×10^8	1.2×10^7	28	22	18	3.4
Iron	7.4×10^{13}	5.6×10^8	132	65	41	0.5
Lead	6.4×10^7	3.1×10^6	21	17	14	–0.5
Nickel	4.6×10^7	1.1×10^6	41	30	22	1.6
Silver	2.8×10^5	1.6×10^4	17	15	13	3.0
Tin	8.0×10^6	2.1×10^5	37	28	21	–0.5
Zinc	1.9×10^8	7.8×10^6	25	20	16	1.9

a. For the metals other than aluminum, reserves are measured in terms of metal content. For aluminum, reserves are measured in terms of bauxite ore.

b. Reserves and primary production are measured in metric tons except for crude oil, which is measured in barrels, and natural gas, which is measured in cubic feet.

c. Life expectancy figures were calculated before reserve and average production data were rounded. As a result, the life expectancies shown in the fourth, fifth, and sixth columns may deviate slightly from the life expectancies derived from the reserve data shown in the second column and the annual primary production data shown in the third column.

Sources: U.S. Bureau of Mines (1977), U.S. Geological Survey (2000a); U.S. Geological Survey (2000b); American Petroleum Institute (2000); BP Amoco (2000); International Energy Agency (2000)

ures for reserves, multiplies them by five, and then presumes that the results provide reasonable estimates of the ultimate availability of various mineral commodities. Others use measures of resources, rather than reserves. Resources encompass reserves plus the quantity of a mineral commodity contained in deposits that are (1) economic but as yet undiscovered, and (2) expected to become economic as a result of new technology or other developments within some foreseeable future. All these attempts, however, suffer from the same fundamental problem as reserves: The resulting figures are ultimately not fixed stocks reflecting the remaining availability of mineral commodities.

Resource Base

Another physical measure, which comes much closer than either reserves or resources to measuring the total amount of various mineral commodities found within the earth, is the *resource base*. This measure encompasses all of a mineral commodity contained in the earth's crust (see Box 3-2). It includes

---

Box 3-2. The Earth's Crust

The earth's crust is the outermost layer of the solid sphere that constitutes the earth. It varies in thickness from 8 to 70 kilometers. It is thinnest beneath the oceans, and does not include the oceans or other bodies of water. Today, magnesium and lithium are profitably produced from seawater. Many other mineral commodities can also be extracted from the oceans, though not profitably, because cheaper sources are available elsewhere. This means that the resource base somewhat underestimates the total amount of mineral commodities found in the upper surface of the earth's sphere.

---

reserves, resources, as well as the contents of all other subsurface occurrences. The resource base does not vary with new discoveries, nor does it change with the prices of mineral commodities or the introduction of new technologies. The relationship among reserves, resources, and the resource base is shown in Figure 3-1, a modification of the well-known McKelvey box.[1]

Table 3-2 shows the resource base for a number of mineral commodities, along with their life expectancies, assuming the demand for primary production grows at 0, 2, and 5 percent annually. The most striking finding is the sheer magnitude of the figures. At current rates of primary exploitation, all

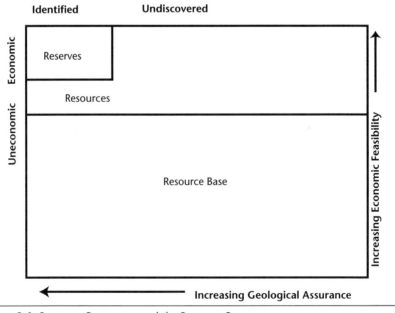

Figure 3-1. Reserves, Resources, and the Resource Base

Table 3-2. Life Expectancies of Resource Base, Selected Mineral Commodities

Mineral Commodity	Resource Base (metric tons)[a]	1997–1999 Average Annual Primary Production	Life Expectancy in Years, at Three Growth Rates in Primary Production			Average Annual Growth in Production, 1975–1999 (percent)
			0%	2%	5%	
Coal[b]	n.a.	4.6×10^9	n.a.	n.a.	n.a.	1.1
Crude oil[b]	n.a.	2.4×10^{10}	n.a.	n.a.	n.a.	0.8
Natural gas[b]	n.a.	8.1×10^{13}	n.a.	n.a.	n.a.	2.9
Aluminum	2.0×10^{18}	2.2×10^7	8.9×10^{10}	1,065	444	2.9
Copper	1.5×10^{15}	1.2×10^7	1.2×10^8	736	313	3.4
Iron	1.4×10^{18}	5.6×10^8	2.5×10^9	886	373	0.5
Lead	2.9×10^{14}	3.1×10^6	9.4×10^6	607	261	–0.5
Nickel	2.1×10^{12}	1.1×10^6	1.8×10^6	526	229	1.6
Silver	1.8×10^{12}	1.6×10^4	1.1×10^8	731	311	3.0
Tin	4.1×10^{13}	2.1×10^5	2.0×10^8	759	322	–0.5
Zinc	2.2×10^{15}	7.8×10^6	2.8×10^8	778	329	1.9

Note: n.a. means not available.

a. The resource base for a mineral commodity is calculated by multiplying its elemental abundance measured in grams per metric ton times the total weight (24×10^{18}) in metric tons of the earth's crust. It reflects the quantity of that material found in the earth's crust.

b. Estimates of the resource base for coal, crude oil, and natural gas do not exist. As a result, data for the resource base and life expectancies for these commodities are not available. The U.S. Geological Survey and other organizations do provide assessments of ultimate recoverable resources for oil, natural gas, and coal. Although these are at times referred to as estimates of the resource base, they do not attempt to measure all the coal, oil, and natural gas found in the earth's crust. As a result, they are more appropriately considered as resource estimates, rather than assessments of the resource base.

Sources: The data on the resource base are based on information in Erickson (1973, 22–23) and Lee and Yao (1970, 778–786). The figures for the 1997–1999 average annual production and the annual percentage growth in production for 1997–1999 are from Table 3-1 and the sources cited there.

the mineral commodities for which we have resource base estimates would last for millions of years, and some for billions of years! Given that our solar system is only about five billion years old and that Homo sapiens has existed as a species for only several hundred thousand years, these are large numbers. They suggest that society might have more pressing problems than mineral depletion.

However, Table 3-2 also shows that assuming a continuous growth in primary production of only two percent annually reduces the life expectancies of the resource base from millions and billions to hundreds and thousands of years. Although these figures are small enough to perhaps cause some concern, like the larger figures they are not very useful indicators of the long-run availability of mineral resources—for four reasons.

First, many mineral commodities, and in particular the metals, are not destroyed as they are extracted and used. Therefore they can be used over and over again. Ignoring the trivial amounts that have been shot into space, the world today has as much copper, lead, and zinc as it ever has had. Some past production of these metals has been degraded and discarded. Recovering and reprocessing this material would be expensive, but this is a matter of costs, not of physical availability.

Second, although recycling is not an option for the energy resources, their ultimate scarcity is constrained by substitution opportunities and backstop alternatives. Coal, natural gas, petroleum, hydropower, uranium, wind, and solar power, for example, can all produce electricity. The mix of these resources in use at any particular time depends largely on their relative costs.

Of course, certain energy resources, such as petroleum, have unique characteristics that at the present time make substitution difficult or impossible in some applications. The automobile with its internal combustion engine, for instance, currently depends on petroleum. However, the opportunities for resource substitution are growing in many important end-use energy applications. Nowhere is this more evident than with the automobile, where new technology is rapidly advancing the prospects for using electricity, fuel cells, and other alternative fuels to power the car of the future. Such alternatives are now technically feasible; their widespread adoption is largely a question of costs.

In light of such substitution opportunities, the depletion of a particular resource poses a problem only if all the alternatives are similarly suffering from growing scarcity. Although the resource base for many of the nonrenewable energy minerals is unknown (and may be smaller or larger than often assumed), the availability of renewable energy resources, particularly solar power, is for all practical purposes unlimited (see Box 3-3).

Third, the resource base ignores the possibility of extracting mineral commodities from beneath the earth's crust or from space. Though such activities seem farfetched at the present time, there are ongoing discussions of mining on the moon and on near-earth asteroids. History suggests that many activities that seem implausible today may be commonplace in a century or two.

Fourth, and perhaps most important, before the world extracts the last drop of oil or the last molecule of silver from the earth's crust, rising costs would completely eradicate demand. This means that economic depletion would threaten the availability of resources long before the physical exhaustion of the resource base would occur.

For these reasons, costs and prices, properly adjusted for inflation, provide a more promising early warning system for long-run resource scarcity than the available physical measures. This brings us to the economic measure of availability.

Box 3-3. The Availability of Solar Power

The availability of solar power reaching the earth's upper atmosphere equals the solar constant times the area of the earth presented to the sun. The solar constant (SC) is the rate of arrival of energy per unit area perpendicular to the sun's rays at earth's location. This equals 1,350 watts per square meter (Giancola 1997). The area of the earth presented to the sun equals πR^2, where R is the radius of the earth (6.38×10^6 meters) and π is the well-known ratio of the circumference of a circle to its diameter (3.14159). So the solar power reaching the upper atmosphere is $SC\ \pi R^2 =$ 1,350 x 3.14159 x $(6.38 \times 10^6)^2 = 1.73 \times 10^{17}$ watts. Because only about 50 percent of this energy reaches the ground (Ristinen and Kraushaar 1998), the total solar power reaching the earth's surface is half of this figure, or 8.6×10^{16} watts. Multiplying this figure by the number of hours in a year (24 x 365) and then dividing by 1,000 (to convert from watts to kilowatts) indicates that 7.9×10^{17} kilowatt-hours of solar energy reach the earth's surface annually.

To comprehend the magnitude of this figure, we can compare it to the energy derived annually from global petroleum production. The amount of energy in a barrel of oil varies. For the United States, it averages about 5.8 million British thermal units (U.S. Energy Information Administration 2001a), or the equivalent of 1.7 thousand kilowatt-hours. As shown in Table 3-1, annual global crude oil production averaged 2.4×10^{10} barrels during the 1997–1999 period. At 1.7 thousand kilowatt-hours per barrel, this output contains 4.0×10^{13} kilowatt-hours of energy, or approximately 0.005 percent of the solar power reaching the earth's surface every year.

According to the U.S. Energy Information Administration (2001b), crude oil production accounts for 40 percent of global energy output. So total energy output currently equals 0.012 percent of the available solar power. This means that the physical availability of solar power is roughly 8,000 times greater than the combined total of the world's current energy production.

The point, it is important to stress, is not to suggest that some day the world may use all of this available solar power. The costs, including the environmental costs, of solar power presumably would rise sufficiently to make the additional use of solar power uneconomic long before the globe was completely smothered with solar panels. The point rather is simply that it is costs, and not physical availability, that ultimately determine the availability of energy commodities.

Economic Measures

There are three widely recognized economic measures of the long-run availability of mineral commodities—the real marginal costs of extraction and processing, the real market price of the mineral commodity, and real user costs (see Box 3-4). As was pointed out in Chapter 2 (see Figure 2-1), mineral commodity producers do not have an incentive to expand output beyond the point at which marginal production costs plus user costs just equal the market price. So these three economic measures are related.

Figure 3-2 illustrates the nature of this relationship. The vertical axis shows the market price for a mineral commodity, and the production costs for the various (discovered) deposits from which mineral companies can produce the commodity. Production costs differ because deposits vary in quality. Some are high grade, easy to process, and located close to cheap ocean transportation with needed infrastructure already in place. Others are not. The column marked A in Figure 3-2 identifies the lowest-cost (highest-quality) deposit. It can produce an output of $0a$ annually at a per-unit cost of C_1. Column B indicates that the next best deposit can produce ab a year at a per-unit cost of C_2. Column C represents the third best deposit, and so on.

The figure indicates that the market price is P and user costs are $P - C_m$ per unit of output. It also assumes that per-unit production costs vary little within any given ore body or deposit, at least in comparison with the differences in costs between deposits. For this reason, production costs are portrayed as a horizontal line for each deposit.

Box 3-4. Real and Nominal Costs and Prices

The nominal costs and prices of mineral commodities may increase over time as a result of inflation, that is, a general rise in the average prices of all goods and services. To remove the effects of inflation, economists and others deflate nominal costs and prices by some measure of inflation, such as the gross domestic product deflator, the consumer price index, and the producer price index. The adjusted figures are referred to as real costs and prices.

For example, if the nominal price of copper rises by 10 percent from one year to the next while inflation increases the average price of all goods and services by 5 percent, the increase in the real price of copper is only 5 percent. Because real costs and prices provide a better measure than nominal costs and prices of the basket of goods and services that must be given up to obtain an additional ton of copper, they more accurately reflect the true trends in the availability of copper and other mineral commodities.

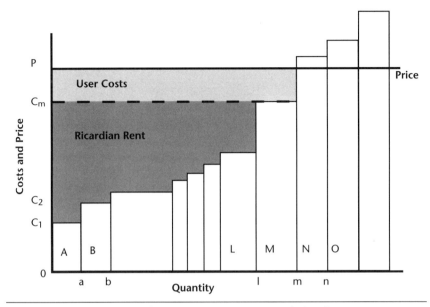

Figure 3-2. Market Price, Production Costs, User Costs, and Ricardian Rent

Assuming that mining companies develop and mine deposits if, and only if, the market price covers their production costs plus user costs, a long-run industry supply curve can be constructed by adding user costs $(P - C_m)$ to the height of each column (the production costs) in Figure 3-2. At the market price P, the industry will produce the output $0m$ from the first M deposits. The ores contained in these deposits are reserves. Columns N and higher represent deposits that are not profitable to exploit at price P. The minerals they contain are resources but not currently reserves.

The production costs plus user costs for deposit M are just equal to the market price, and it is this deposit that illustrates the relationship among market price, marginal production costs, and user costs—our three economic measures of resource availability. Intramarginal deposits, those in categories A through L, enjoy production costs plus user costs that are lower than the market price, and so they earn an additional profit as a result of their superior quality. This extra profit, as was noted in Chapter 2, is commonly called Ricardian rent (see Box 3-5). As Figure 3-2 shows, although only deposits A through L enjoy Ricardian rent, they as well as deposit M are compensated for their user costs.

In contrast, the user costs shown in Figure 3-2 are not true economic rents, though often economists and others refer to user costs as Hotelling rents or as scarcity rent. Though deposits A through L can lose their Ricardian rent and their owners still have an incentive to remain in production, this is not the case of deposits that are no longer able to recover their user costs. Any fall in

---

Box 3-5. Economic Rents, Ricardian Rent, and User Costs

For most people, rent is simply the payment made to the landlord, usually at the beginning of the month, for an apartment or house. For economists, however, the term has a quite different and very special meaning.

A rent is a payment to the owner of a factor of production—such as an employee or worker in the case of labor or an owner of the mineral rights in the case of a mineral deposit—beyond that required by the owner to offer the factor of production he or she controls to the market. A football player, for example, with a salary of $1,000,000 a year, earns a rent of $900,000 if he otherwise would have to work as an electrical engineer at an annual salary of $100,000 (assuming he did not favor one of the positions for reasons other than salary). Similarly, firms, which can be thought of as a collection of factors of production, earn rents when they receive a price above that needed to effect their entry into the industry (of if they are already in the industry to prevent their exit).

The Ricardian rent shown in Figure 3-2 for deposits A through L is a particular type of economic rent. It indicates how much the price of the mineral commodity could fall before these deposits would cease their production.

---

price, for example, would encourage deposit M to shut down. This is because user costs represent costs, not rents. For this reason, we favor the term *user costs* over either Hotelling rents or scarcity rents.

Although Figure 3-2 highlights the relationship among price, costs, and user costs, these three indicators of resource availability measure different things. The market price reflects the opportunity cost (in the sense of what has to be given up) of obtaining another unit of the mineral commodity—a barrel of crude oil or a ton of refined copper, for example.

User costs reflect the value of the oil or copper ore in the ground. Under certain conditions, user costs approximate the expected costs also of finding one more unit of marginal quality (category M) reserves.[2] Higher-quality reserves normally are more costly to discover, because fewer of these deposits are likely to exist and presumably a greater portion of those that do exist have already been found. Their expected discovery costs approximate user costs plus the associated Ricardian rent.

Extraction and processing costs reflect the value of the labor and other inputs required to extract resources from the ground and to convert them into crude oil, refined copper, or other mineral commodities ready to be sold in the marketplace. These differences mean that the three economic measures may provide different signals regarding the long-run availability of mineral commodities.

In a static world where no discovery or new technology occurs and where the existing ore is all of the same quality, Hotelling (1931) has shown that user costs rise at r percent a year (the rate of return on other assets similar to mineral resources in the ground).[3] Extraction and processing costs remain constant. As a result, the marginal cost of producing the last unit of output is the same for each period, and equals the average costs across all output. In this situation, the market price rises at the same absolute rate as the user costs. Unless extraction and processing costs are zero, however, the increase in the market price is less than r percent, the rate for user costs. In this situation, user costs and to a lesser extent market prices indicate growing scarcity, while production costs show no change in resource availability.

Allowing for technological change in the extraction and processing of mineral commodities introduces the possibility that production costs may decline over time. Such a decline may more than offset the rise in user costs, allowing the market price to decline. This favorable trend cannot continue indefinitely, however, because over time user costs account for a growing portion of the market price. As Chapter 4 will explain, this possibility has led Slade and others to hypothesize that real mineral commodity prices follow a U-shaped curve over time, first declining and then rising.

Going one step further—and allowing not only for technological change in extraction and processing but also for new discoveries and mineral deposits of varying qualities—introduces the possibility that user costs as well as production costs may fall over time, permitting the market price to decline indefinitely. To illustrate this possibility, consider Figure 3-2 once again and assume that there are many large deposits with the same production costs as deposit N. In this case, production costs, once they reached those of deposit N, would stabilize. User costs would shift downward, because the lost future profits associated with increased output today would not arise for many years, when deposit N and all other similar deposits were exhausted. As a result, the present value of these lost profits would likely be far lower than the present value of the lost future profits associated with increasing current production prior to the exploitation of deposit N.

Such situations may arise where backstop technologies exist. Should the cost of producing natural gas, for example, rise sufficiently so that solar energy becomes economic, the user costs associated with energy production from natural gas would fall to zero.

Challenges to Economic Measures

Our economic measures (price, marginal production costs, and user costs) of mineral resource availability are now widely (though not universally) accepted as superior to the physical measures (reserves, resources, and the resource base). They are not perfect, however. Mineral commodity prices, for example, may at least in the short run be more influenced by cyclical fluctuations in the business cycle, accidents, strikes, and other factors than trends in long-run availability. They can also be distorted by a variety of market imperfections, including cartels and other forms of market power, government price controls, public subsidies, and environmental and other social costs that producers and consumers do not pay. The sharp rise in oil prices in the early 1970s, for example, reflected more the actual or perceived market power of the Organization of the Petroleum Exporting Countries and short-run fluctuations in the business cycle than rising long-run availability problems.

Similarly, market imperfections and disturbances, again particularly in the short run, may distort extraction costs on the margin. The jump in oil prices in the early 1970s, for example, stimulated investors to develop high-cost wells that previously were uneconomic. An additional shortcoming of extraction costs is their failure to anticipate the future. Although current mineral commodity prices will rise in anticipation of future shortages, extraction costs depend on the quality of the resources currently being used rather than the quality of those the future will use.

User costs are particularly easy to interpret when extraction costs are constant. When extraction costs are rising, however, we have seen that user costs can decline as society moves to poorer quality but more abundant resources. This reflects a reduction in the future threat of resource shortages, but does not reflect past trends very well. If trends in extraction costs focus too much on the past, trends in user costs suffer from the opposite tendency.

Another shortcoming of our economic measures of scarcity is that they can provide quite different indications of resource availability trends. New technology, for example, may over time drive production costs down while depletion may be pushing user costs up. Mineral commodity prices in such situations may be rising, falling, or constant, and the implications for trends in mineral commodity availability are ambiguous.

Ecological economists and others also challenge the use of our economic indicators on the grounds that they are mere reflections of an inadequate, and in some respects fundamentally flawed, market process. Here the case against economic measures encompasses at least five concerns.

First, the economic system, it is argued, is just a part or a subsystem of a finite global ecosystem. The economic system extracts resources from and jettisons waste back into the ecosystem. While the world economy was small, the ecosystem absorbed these interactions with little or no costs. With the growth of the global economic system during the past century, however, this has changed, and as a result large environmental and social costs associated with current economic activities are not reflected in the costs that producers incur or the prices that consumers pay. In a debate with Julian Simon, Norman Myers advanced this view:

> The goods we purchase have often been produced at a concealed cost of pollution during the production process, and when we consume them or throw them away after use, still more pollution ensues, for instance, acid rain, ozone-layer depletion, and global warming. This is pollution for everybody today and tomorrow, not just for the purchaser. Yet the social costs are far from reflected in the prices we pay: the economic externalities are rarely internalized, even though they should be if prices are to serve as realistic indicators. Externalities are nothing less than larcenous costs imposed on other people. (Myers and Simon 1994, 185)

Traditional economists would agree that all costs—including the environmental and other social costs—of producing mineral commodities should be internalized if prices and costs are to reflect true trends in resource availability. The critics, however, believe that external costs are very large and pervasive. They question whether society has the ability or the will to force producers and consumers to pay these costs. They also contend that the prices and costs recorded for mineral commodities in the past would be much higher and increasing much faster if these costs were taken into account.

Second, the marketplace provides reliable indicators of scarcity only if participants determining mineral commodity prices, extraction costs, and user costs are themselves properly informed. As Norgaard (1990, 19–20) has suggested: "If resource allocators are not informed, the cost and price paths their decisions generate are as likely to reflect their ignorance as reality."

Third, a small percentage of the world's population unduly determines the demand for mineral commodities due to the very skewed distribution of global income and wealth. Again, according to Myers:

> In any case, market indicators . . . reflect the evaluation only of those people who can register their money votes in the marketplace—an option that, as we have seen, is almost entirely denied to two people out of five worldwide. What would be these people's reaction to . . . assurances that spending power is steadily enhanced through declining prices—or that the Waldorf [a luxury hotel in New York City] is increasingly open to all?

Such distortions in demand bias the trajectories of prices and the other economic indicators of resources availability. A more equitable distribution of income and wealth would allow the bottom third of the world's population to increase greatly their demand for housing, food, and other basic necessities. Of course, the richest third would have to reduce its demand for goods and services, but overall such a transformation would likely increase appreciably the world's appetite for materials and energy. This in turn would generate a different, perhaps very different, pattern of mineral commodity prices and production costs than that produced by the highly inequitable market system that currently exists.

Fourth, the market system also fails to give adequate weight to the interests of future generations, because it is the living alone (and not their yet-to-be-born descendents) who interact in the marketplace and shape the public policies that determine commodity prices. If the voices of future generations were taken into account, the critics claim, we would discount future profits less and raise current commodity prices in order to tilt the consumption of resources more toward the future.

Fifth, the marketplace takes into account only the interests of people. Yet other species, it is argued, have intrinsic value as well. The market and public policy consider their interests only to the extent that people are prepared to champion them. This anthropocentric focus, like the focus on the current generation, raises the possibility that both the level and trends in commodity prices might be far higher if the welfare of all living creatures, rather than just people, were properly considered.

These challenges to the economic measures of resource availability raise important issues, which deserve more attention. The first contends that the true costs of mineral production (and many other economic activities) far exceed the costs that producers incur and in turn the prices that consumers pay. This implies a massive failure of public policy to internalize environmental and other social costs. Few would argue that public policy is perfect. Vested interests and widespread ignorance can and often do promote suboptimal policies. The issue here, however, is how convincing a case can be made for a massive failure of public policy over an extended period of time, particularly for those countries where governments are ultimately accountable to their citizens.

The second concern—that the ignorance of market participants cripples our economic measures of resource availability—highlights the complications introduced by uncertainty and imperfect information. To what extent these complications undermine the usefulness of economic measures, however, depends on (1) the use to which they are put and (2) the pervasiveness of the ignorance. If the objective is to forecast accurately on the basis of current indicators, and if one believes that current participants in the marketplace are ill informed, then the economic measures are of questionable use. But if current participants are thought to be reasonably savvy, particularly because the market provides them with considerable incentive to become informed, one should have more confidence in the trends portrayed by economic measures.

In either case, as Krautkraemer (1998, 2088) points out, economic indicators reflect the "available information about scarcity at a particular time and that information changes over time." So economic indicators should reflect the collective wisdom of the market about how resource scarcity is changing. Although this collective wisdom is imperfect, the critical question is whether it runs counter to the best evidence available on future resource scarcity over an extended period of time.

The other challenges to the economic measures of resource availability raise even more fundamental philosophical issues, regarding not just how to measure resource availability but, more important, the values we hold individually and collectively as a society, and thus consider when allocating resources and making decisions. Ultimately, however, these challenges are relevant only to the extent that they influence those individuals whose decisions and behavior matter, as the following quote from Stokey and Zeckhauser (1978, 262) so colorfully argues:

> Our main point is that it's people, and only people, that count. This means that redwoods and bluebirds and Lake Baikal and the Old Man of the Mountain are worth saving only if people believe them worth saving. Abstractly considered, the rights of nonhuman entities may seem a valid criterion for policy. But in fact these rights are meaningless unless championed by people; neither the redwoods nor the bluebirds can speak for themselves. If this judgment strikes you as unduly hard-nosed, look at the other side of the coin. How many voices are raised on behalf of that vanishing species, the smallpox virus? And who speaks for the boll weevil? There is ample pragmatic support for an anthropocentric approach. All philosophical justifications to the contrary, unless human beings care about redwoods, the redwoods will be destroyed.

Although many thoughtful individuals would like to see a more equitable distribution of global income and wealth, it matters little for resource availability (or anything else for that matter) until such concerns actually affect the purchasing power of the economically disenfranchised. Similarly, the interests of future generations or of other species, regardless of the arguments on their behalf, affect the present only to the extent that the current generation of humans takes them into account. To say that trends in resource availability would have been less favorable if public policy had been different (better) may be interesting, but it in no way alters the actual trends. Gasoline burns in a luxury Cadillac or a small Honda, in a sport utility vehicle or a moped—and there is no way now to alter past patterns of use.

Notes

1. Vincent E. McKelvey, a geologist and former director of the U.S. Geological Survey, developed a widely used resource classification scheme (McKelvey 1973), which became

known as the McKelvey box. The McKelvey box is similar to Figure 3-1, except that it excludes the resource base, because many geologists including McKelvey believe that mineral resources that are not reserves or resources are of little or no practical interest.

2. This follows when firms have an incentive to expand their exploration efforts up to the point where the expected cost of finding another unit of reserves just equals the value of that unit.

3. Where capacity constrains the production of mineral commodities, Cairns (2001) shows that the r percent rule applies only if user costs include the shadow value of capital. For this and other reasons, r percent provides only an upper limit on the rise in user costs over time.

References

American Petroleum Institute. 2000. *Basic Petroleum Data Book*. Washington, DC: American Petroleum Institute.

BP Amoco. 2000. *BP Amoco Statistical Review of World Energy 2000*. London: British Petroleum Company.

Cairns, R.D. 2001. Capacity Choice and the Theory of the Mine. *Environmental and Resource Economics* 18: 129–148.

Erickson, R.L. 1973. Crustal Abundance of Elements, and Mineral Reserves and Resources. In *United States Mineral Resources*, Geological Survey Professional Paper 820, edited by D.A. Brobst and W.P. Pratt. Washington, DC: Government Printing Office, 21–25.

Giancola, D.C. 1997. *Physics*. Upper Saddle River, NJ: Prentice Hall.

Hotelling, H. 1931. The Economics of Exhaustible Resources. *Journal of Political Economy* 39(2): 137–175.

International Energy Agency. 2000. *Oil, Gas, Coal and Electricity Quarterly Statistics, Second Quarter*. Paris: International Energy Agency.

Krautkraemer, J.A. 1998. Nonrenewable Resource Scarcity. *Journal of Economic Literature* 36: 2065–2107.

Lee, T., and C.-L. Yao. 1970. Abundance of Chemical Elements in the Earth's Crust and Its Major Tectonic Units. *International Geological Review* 12(7): 778–786.

McKelvey, V.E. 1973. Mineral Resource Estimates and Public Policy. In *United States Mineral Resources*, Geological Survey Professional Paper 820, edited by D.A. Brobst and W.P. Pratt. Washington, DC: Government Printing Office, 9–19. This article also appears in *American Scientist* 60: 32–40.

Meadows, D.H., and others. 1972. *The Limits to Growth*. New York: Universe Books.

Myers, N., and J.L. Simon. 1994. *Scarcity or Abundance? A Debate on the Environment*. New York: Norton.

Norgaard, R.B. 1990. Economic Indicators of Resource Scarcity: A Critical Essay. *Journal of Environmental Economics and Management* 19: 19–25.

Ristinen, R.A., and J.J. Kraushaar. 1998. *Energy and the Environment*. New York: Wiley.

Slade, M.E. 1982. Trends in Natural-Resource Commodity Prices: An Analysis of the Time Domain. *Journal of Environmental Economics and Management* 9: 122–137.

Stokey, E., and R. Zeckhauser. 1978. *A Primer for Policy Analysis*. New York: Norton.

U.S. Bureau of Mines. 1977. *Commodity Data Summaries 1977*. Washington, DC: U.S. Bureau of Mines.

U.S. Energy Information Administration, Department of Energy. 2001a. Gross Heat Content of Crude Oil, 1990–1999. http://www.eia.doe.gov/emeu/iea/table c3.html

———. 2001b. World Consumption of Primary Energy by Selected Country Groups (Btu), 1990–1999. http://www/eia/doe/gov/emeu/iea/table18.html

U.S. Geological Survey. 2000a. *Mineral Commodity Summaries Online 2000.* http://minerals.usgs.gov/minerals/pubs/mcs/

———. 2000b. *Minerals Yearbook: Volume I, Metals and Minerals.* http://minerals.usgs.gov/minerals/pubs/commodity/myb/

Chapter 4

The Benevolent Past

This chapter looks backward, to the end of the nineteenth century and the beginning of the twentieth century. It examines the research others have conducted to identify the historical trends in resource availability during this period, research that begins with the 1870s and then runs through the intervening years to the present. Ultimately, we are concerned about the future, not the past, and past trends, of course, may not continue into the future. Nevertheless, an understanding of the past will prove useful when we turn our attention toward the future in Chapter 5.

This chapter is organized around our three economic measures of resource availability. It looks first at trends in the real costs of producing mineral products, then at trends in real mineral commodity prices, and finally at trends in real user costs. The last section draws some general conclusions about past trends in resource availability and explains some of the inconsistencies among the three measures.

Production Costs

Mineral-producing companies do not generally make their production costs available to the public. Some consulting firms, government agencies, and even producing companies collect and estimate this information, primarily for what are called *cash costs* (which approximate variable costs, and thus exclude capital costs).[1] These series, however, go back at best only several decades.

As a result, efforts to measure production costs have focused on trends in the inputs used to produce mineral commodities. This, for example, is the approach taken by Barnett and Morse (1963) in their pioneering book *Scarcity and Growth*, which was mentioned in Chapter 2. Using data compiled by Potter and Christy (1962) and Kendrick (1961), they construct indices of the labor used per unit of output and of the labor plus capital used per unit of output for all extractive industries. They also compute the same indices for agriculture, for minerals, for forestry, and for a number of specific industries within these economic sectors. Their study, which looks just at the United States, covers the period from 1870 to 1957.

Because we measure the availability of oil or any other mineral commodity by the basket of goods and services that society must forgo to obtain another unit, the use of physical measures of inputs—labor and capital in the case of Barnett and Morse—provides an incomplete picture of availability trends. When the prices of inputs rise, as was clearly the case for real wages during the period that Barnett and Morse examine, the results underestimate the decline or overestimate the increase in availability. When the prices of inputs decline, just the opposite is true.

It is also important to note that Barnett and Morse measure the average labor and capital costs of resource production across all producers, and not the costs of marginal producers (as one would ideally like). As a result, they tend to underestimate the labor and capital required by marginal producers. This, however, may not greatly affect their results and findings. Because they are looking at trends over time, trends in an index of average costs may closely track the trends in an index of marginal costs.

Table 4-1 shows their results when production costs are measured in terms of labor and capital inputs per unit of output. At the time the Barnett and Morse study appeared, these results created some surprise. They indicate that the labor and capital inputs needed to produce extractive resources in general declined dramatically—by more than 50 percent—during the nearly 90-year period examined, despite the dramatic growth in their consumption. Moreover, the pace of decline was greater after 1919 than before, suggesting not only that resources were becoming more available over time, but that they were doing so at an accelerating rate. Finally, the fall in production costs was even greater for the mineral sector—more than 75 percent—although this sector relies upon nonrenewable resources, unlike agriculture and forestry.

When Barnett and Morse separate the mineral sector into the mineral fuels, the metals, and the nonmetals, they find that all three of these groups experienced substantial declines in production costs (measured in terms of labor input per unit of output). When these three groups are further broken down into individual mineral commodities, the decreasing trend continues to be pervasive. Petroleum and natural gas, bituminous and anthracite coal, iron

Table 4-1. Indices of Labor and Capital Inputs per Unit of Output for All U.S. Extractive Industries and for the Agriculture, Minerals, and Forestry Sectors, 1870–1957 (1929 = 100)

Period or Year	All Extractive Industries	Agriculture	Minerals	Forestry
1870–1900	134	132	210	59
1919	122	114	164	106
1957	60	61	47	90

Source: Barnett and Morse 1963, 8.

ore, copper, phosphate rock, stone, fluorspar, sulfur, and other mineral commodities all require less labor input per unit of output as time passes.

Barnett and Morse attribute these favorable trends largely to technological change. New technologies lower the costs of finding new resources. New technologies allow the exploitation of previously known but uneconomic resources. New technologies permit the substitution of less scarce resources for scarcer resources. New technology reduces the quantity of resources needed to produce final goods and services.

Moreover, Barnett and Morse do not believe such innovations are just fortunate random events, but rather are driven by need. So they can be counted on to continue in the future to enhance resource availability. In their own words:

> These developments . . . are not essentially fortuitous. At one time they were, but important changes have occurred in man's knowledge of the physical universe over the past two centuries, changes which have built technological advance into the social processes of the modern world. . . . Not only ingenuity but, increasingly, understanding; not luck but systematic investigation, are turning the tables on nature, making her subservient to man. And the signals that channel research effort, now in one direction, now in another—that determine innovational priorities—are usually the problems calling loudest to be solved. Sometimes the signals are political and social. More often, in a private enterprise society, they are market forces. (Barnett and Morse 1963, 9–10)

The Barnett and Morse study, in large part because of its surprising findings, did not go unchallenged. Indeed, the study fostered a wave of research on resource extraction and processing costs that continues down to the present. Some writers (Cleveland 1991) question the focus on just labor and capital inputs, arguing the results might be quite different if energy and other inputs were also taken into account. Energy is an important input for the extraction, processing, and transportation of many mineral commodities, particularly the metals. Electricity, for example, can alone account for more than 25 percent of the costs of smelting aluminum (Nappi 1988, Table 7-3).

Other critics, including Barnett (1979) himself, raise the possibility that production costs could be falling in the United States, thanks to its increasing reliance on imports, while rising for the world as a whole. Still others note that the rising environmental costs associated with resource production were not included in their figures. Finally, some commentators (Johnson and others 1980; Hall and Hall 1984) claim that extending the Barnett and Morse analysis beyond 1957 might uncover a reversal in the downward cost trend.

Although all the above are legitimate concerns, the Barnett and Morse results have proven remarkably robust. Subsequent research (Barnett 1979; Johnson and others 1980; Slade 1988, 1992; Uri and Boyd 1995) on the costs of resource extraction has for the most part supported the Barnett and Morse conclusion that production costs have fallen since the late 1800s for resources in general, and particularly so for nonrenewable mineral resources.[2]

Mineral Commodity Prices

Mineral commodity prices enjoy two important practical advantages over the two other economic indicators of resource availability. First, they are readily available and easy to obtain. Second, they are reasonably reliable. This is particularly true for mineral prices set on commodity exchanges, such as the London Metal Market. As a result, there is a rich history of studies of mineral commodity prices.

This section looks first at the early studies undertaken in the 1960s and 1970s. It then focuses on the attempts to model the historical trends in mineral commodity prices that began in the 1980s. These early modeling efforts in turn fostered a number of more sophisticated models, in some instances employing new advances in time-series analysis. They are considered toward the end of the chapter.

Early Efforts

Potter and Christy (1962) provide one of the first systematic analyses of price trends for natural resource commodities. Their work covers a variety of agricultural, mineral, and forestry products in the United States. It spans the period 1870 to 1957, and was subsequently updated to 1973 by Manthy (1978). Nominal prices are converted to real prices by using the U.S. producer price index (PPI) to adjust for inflation.[3]

Figure 4-1, reproduced from Potter and Christy, shows the long-run price trends for all resources, and for the agricultural, mineral, and forestry sectors separately. It indicates that mineral prices fell by more than 40 percent between 1870 and 1957. All of this decline, however, took place during the first decade of this period. After 1880, mineral prices displayed considerable

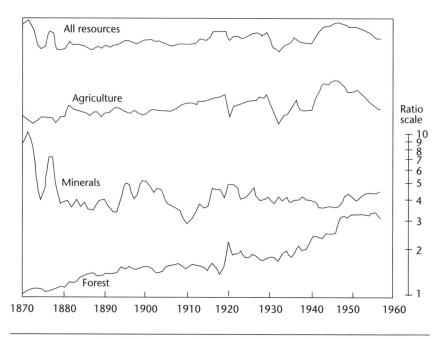

Figure 4-1. Real Prices for All Resources and for the Agriculture, Minerals, and Forest Sectors

Note: This figure uses a logarithmic scale to measure prices, which gives equal value to equal percentage changes in price. This allows an easy comparison of price series of completely different magnitude.

Source: Potter and Christy 1962, Chart 1.

short-term fluctuations in response to wars and other disturbances, but changed little over the long term.

The data for all minerals, however, hide major differences in price trends among individual commodities. For example, the real prices of coal, lead, and lime rose during the 1870–1957 period, whereas those for iron, zinc, copper, petroleum, and phosphate rock fell.[4]

Barnett and Morse (1963) also examine the price data collected by Potter and Christy, deflating these data by the prices of nonextractive goods, rather than the PPI. Abstracting from short-run movements, they find that mineral prices have remained quite constant since the last quarter of the nineteenth century. These findings are similar to those of Potter and Christy, and stand in sharp contrast to the dramatic decline Barnett and Morse find in the production costs of mineral commodities during the same period.[5] Nor do they suggest an acceleration in the rate at which availability is increasing, as is the case for their production cost data. Nevertheless, Barnett and Morse contend that trends in prices like those for production costs provide no support for the hypothesis that mineral depletion is causing resource scarcity.

Writing a decade later, Nordhaus (1974) does find substantial declines in the long-run price trends for many important mineral commodities. Between 1900 and 1970, for example, his work shows a price drop of 97 percent for aluminum; 90 percent for petroleum; 87 percent for copper, lead, and zinc; 84 percent for iron; and 78 percent for coal. Nordhaus uses the cost of labor to deflate the prices of mineral commodities, which largely explains why his results differ from those of Potter and Christy and of Barnett and Morse. Over the years, labor costs have risen much more rapidly than the prices of wholesale goods or of nonextractive goods.

These findings highlight the fact that long-run price trends may vary depending on the deflator used to adjust for inflation. Nordhaus's deflator—labor costs—has the advantage of showing trends in the number of hours of labor that one could buy for the price of various mineral commodities, a measure of opportunity costs that is easy to comprehend. Conversely, labor costs have risen in part because investments in human capital (more education, improvements in on-the-job training, better health care) have enhanced the quality of labor. For this reason, the price trends identified by Potter and Christy and by Barnett and Morse are a better measure of the trends in mineral commodity availability.

Econometric Models

Smith (1979) provides one of the earliest attempts to model mineral price trends. Relying primarily on the data of Potter and Christy (1962), as updated and modified by Manthy (1978), he postulates the following simple linear time trend over the 1900–1973 period for the real prices of four categories of natural resources (total extractive goods, mineral commodities, forestry products, and agricultural goods):

$$P_t = \alpha_0 + \alpha_1 t + \varepsilon_t \qquad\qquad 4\text{-}1$$

where P_t is the average price in year t for each of the natural resource categories deflated by the U.S. producer price index; t is the time trend ($t = 1, 2, \ldots$ 74); ε_t is the disturbance term[6] in year t; and α_0 and α_1 are unknown parameters, which are assumed to remain constant during the period. The parameter α_0 indicates the expected price for the time period just before the analysis begins (when $t = 0$), and so should be positive. The parameter α_1 determines the slope of the price trend line. It is positive, zero, or negative depending on whether the long-run trend in prices is rising, horizontal, or falling.

Smith uses regression analysis to estimate the parameters, and he finds that the estimates for the parameter of the trend variable (α_1) are statistically significant (in the sense that they differ from zero with a probability of 90 percent or more) only in the case of forest products. These results at first blush appear to support the conclusions of Potter and Christy and of Barnett and Morse that aside from the forestry sector there has been no significant trend over the long term in the real prices of natural resource products.

Smith, however, argues that this conclusion is warranted only if the parameters in his model (α_0, α_1) remain constant during the entire 1900–1973 period. Using two alternative statistical techniques,[7] he shows that this is highly unlikely. In the case of minerals, his findings suggest that the estimate for the time trend parameter (α_1) was negative and rising toward zero during the decade from 1910 to 1920, implying that prices were falling during this period but at a slower and slower pace. The time trend parameter then turns positive during the 1920s and 1930s, implying that prices were rising during these years. It becomes negative again during the 1940s, 1950s, and early 1960s, and thereafter remains very close to zero until 1973, the end of the period examined.

These findings, he suggests, should not be surprising. During the years 1900–1973, many changes affecting resource price trends were occurring. The nature of the U.S. economy was evolving, causing substantial shifts in the relative importance of individual commodities within the aggregate categories. Petroleum, for example, was becoming much more important both within the mineral sector and within the extractive goods sector as a whole.

As a result of such developments, Smith contends, the trends that real resource prices followed changed during the 1900–1973 period. So the failure of resource prices to rise in the long run may obscure more recent evidence covering a shorter period of time that reflects growing resource scarcity. For this reason, he questions the conclusions of Potter and Christy and of Barnett and Morse.

Slade (1982), in an influential empirical study, argues that the true relation between real resource prices and time is U-shaped.[8] In support of this hypothesis, she notes that the prices for mineral commodities should, under competitive market conditions, equal their marginal production costs plus user costs (as shown in Figures 2-1 and 3-2).

User costs, according to Hotelling (as we saw in Chapter 2), should be increasing over time. Production costs, however, may be rising or falling. Slade contends that technological change tends to push extraction and processing costs down over time, whereas the need to exploit lower-grade and poorer-quality deposits tends to drive production costs up. For a time, the beneficial effects of technological change may offset the adverse effects of poorer-quality deposits as well as the rise in user costs. In this case, production costs will fall by more than user costs rise, allowing the real price to decline.

This favorable trend, however, cannot continue indefinitely. Over time, production costs account for a smaller and smaller share of the sum of production costs and user costs, and so the rise in user costs must eventually offset the decline in production costs. Slade believes this reversal will be reinforced by natural limits on new technology that eventually will cause even production costs to rise.

Figure 4-2 portrays the expected scenario. At the beginning of the period under analysis (T_0), user costs are quite small in comparison with marginal production costs. Early in the period, thanks to technological change, production costs fall sufficiently to offset the upward trend in user costs. This favorable trend continues until time T_1, after which the rise in user costs exceeds the decline in production costs, causing the price to rise. Eventually, at time T_2, the downward trend in production costs is also reversed as the rise in costs caused by the decline in ore grade and deposit quality offsets the effects of new technology.

Slade tests this hypothesis for 11 important mineral commodities—3 fuels (coal, natural gas, and petroleum) and 8 metals (aluminum, copper, iron, lead, nickel, silver, tin, and zinc). She assumes the hypothesized U-shaped relationship between price and time can be captured by the quadratic function

$$P_t = \alpha_0 + \alpha_1 t + \alpha_2 t^2 + \varepsilon_t \qquad\qquad 4\text{-}2$$

where P_t is the average price in year t for each of the 11 mineral commodities deflated by the U.S. producer price index; t is the time trend ($t = 1, 2, \ldots$); ε_t is the disturbance term in year t; and α_0, α_1, and α_2 are unknown parameters.

For each commodity, Slade uses price data from 1870 (or the first year for which data are available) to 1978 and regression analysis to estimate the parameters (α_0, α_1, α_2) of equation 4-2. For comparative purposes, she also estimates the linear relationship, shown in equation 4-1, between prices and time.

Her assumed U-shaped relationship between prices and time anticipates that the estimate for α_1 will be negative and the estimate for α_2 will be positive, a result that she finds holds for all 11 mineral commodities. Moreover, except for lead, the estimates for α_2, which indicate a nonlinear relationship, are positive at probability levels that exceed 90 percent. These results support Slade's hypothesis that mineral prices tend to fall and then rise over time. Moreover, in all cases she finds that the minimum point on the estimated relationship between price and time is reached before 1973. This, she concludes, "indicates that nonrenewable natural-resource commodities are becoming scarce" (Slade 1982, 136).[9]

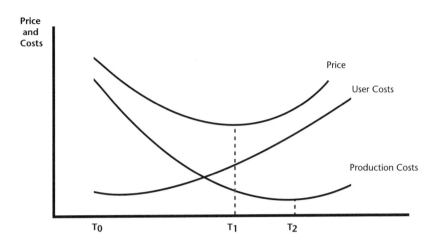

Figure 4-2. Hypothesized Trends in User Costs, Marginal Production Costs, and Prices for Mineral Commodities

Source: A modification of Figure 1 in Slade 1982.

Recent Developments

In large part because of its important implications for the long-run availability of mineral commodities, Slade's study has received considerable attention. Subsequent studies have raised five concerns or caveats about her analysis.

First, as we saw above, Smith questions whether one can assume the parameters of the simple linear model are constant over time. The same question can be raised for Slade's quadratic relationship.

In her article, Slade (1982, 129, 136) actually addresses this issue in passing. If the true relation is, as she assumes, a quadratic function, with prices first declining but eventually rising, Smith should find the estimated parameter on the time variable in his linear equation is negative in the early years of his sample, but declining toward zero. Eventually, it should turn positive, as real prices bottom out and start to increase. Slade claims that this is what Smith's results show.

A close look at his results for the mineral sector indicates that this is true for the period up to 1920, but not thereafter. This is not what we would expect if the quadratic equation with invariant parameters applied over the entire 1870–1978 period that Slade examines. Berck (1995) and Pindyck (1999) provide further evidence that the long-run relationship between mineral prices and time changes over time.

This is troubling, for it suggests that efforts to estimate empirically such relations are shooting at moving targets. Any given effort, particularly if it covers a long span of time, is likely to estimate a hybrid curve that reflects several different true relationships, each relevant during different periods with no guarantee that the estimated results even closely approximate the current long-run relationship.

Second, a related challenge comes from modern time-series analysis, much of which was not available to Slade in the early 1980s when she wrote her original article. The statistical properties of her results, which so strongly support her hypothesis regarding the long-run trend in mineral prices, depend on mineral prices being what is called *trend stationary*. This means that the prices of mineral commodities will revert back to the same long-run trends if disturbed by a short-run shock, such as a strike or a war. If this is not the case, then prices follow a *stochastic trend*, and the parameters (α_0, α_1, α_2) change during the period examined in response to short-run shocks.

Several scholars (Agbeyegbe 1993; Berck and Roberts 1996; Ahrens and Sharma 1997; Howie 2001), including Slade (1988), have subsequently carried out tests to determine if the price series for the mineral commodities she considers are trend stationary. The results vary; in some cases they indicate that the trends are stationary, in other cases that they are stochastic.

Third, Slade's analysis ends in 1978. As Krautkraemer (1998) shows in some detail, the prices for many energy and other mineral commodities fell during the 1980s and 1990s. This raises the possibility that her findings might be quite different if the study were carried out today.

Howie (2001) has recently updated Slade's data, and the results are shown in the Appendix to the present volume. He also reestimates her equations, using the same regression techniques (as well as more modern time-series techniques) and the same set of commodities. In addition to the linear and quadratic relationships, he considers the possibility that prices follow an inverse trend in the long run. He finds that the linear trend best describes lead and petroleum prices; the inverse trend, aluminum, copper, and zinc prices; and the quadratic trend, only nickel prices.[10] He also concludes that the price trends for bituminous coal, iron ore, pig iron, natural gas, silver, and tin may be stochastic, rather than stationary, which calls into question the estimated results for these commodities.

Fourth, like most other scholars analyzing long-run price trends, Slade assumes that a commodity's price equals its marginal production cost plus user costs. Implicitly, she and others assume that the marginal production costs reflected in prices are those that prevail in the long run, not the short run, for long-run production costs are what are relevant for measuring the long-run availability of mineral commodities.

Yet in the short run (a period so short that firms cannot change their capacity), when the economy is booming and the demand for mineral commodities is strong, marginal production costs can for a time far exceed their long-run levels. Conversely, when the economy is depressed and the mineral industries are suffering from excess capacity, marginal production costs are likely to fall below their long-run levels. By examining mineral prices over a number of decades, Slade and others presume that such short-run deviations of production costs and prices from their long-run values more or less cancel out.

Another potential problem arises when prices are not the outcome of the interaction of supply and demand in a competitive market. This can occur when producers acting individually or collusively exercise market power and control the market price. It can also occur during wars and other emergencies, when governments impose price controls on mineral commodities. Such market distortions have occurred with some frequency in the past, as Figure 4-3 illustrates for copper. During such periods, price is a biased indicator of availability, overestimating scarcity when cartels and other collusive activities maintain the price at artificially high levels and underestimating scarcity when price controls keep prices from reaching their market-clearing levels.

Slade (1982, n. 14) raises the possibility that the Organization of the Petroleum Exporting Countries (OPEC) cartel and the increases in energy prices it produced after 1973 might account for the subsequent upturn in mineral prices. She dismisses this possibility, however, by noting that the estimated curves for all of the mineral commodities she examines reached their minimum point before 1973.

Although the general public is well aware of OPEC's efforts to control the price of oil since 1973, less well known are the frequent attempts to control the price of copper, nickel, tin, and numerous other mineral commodities during the past century. Most of these efforts lasted for only a few years, and like the short-run impact of the business cycle on prices, there is some tendency for the effects of market power on price to cancel out in the long run.[11] For example, the sharp increases in oil prices during the 1970s encouraged new sources of supply and a reduction in demand that caused real oil prices to decline during much of the 1980s. Similarly, the artificially high price for tin that the International Tin Agreement managed to sustain for two decades eventually led to its spectacular collapse in 1985. For the next 5 to 10 years, the price of tin was severely depressed by the additions to capacity and the reductions in demand that the high price encouraged during the earlier period (Rogers 1992).

The available literature, unfortunately, provides few studies that systematically examine how—if at all—market power alters the long-run trends in commodity prices. We do know that during the past century many nonfuel mineral markets have become more competitive as the costs of transporting bulk

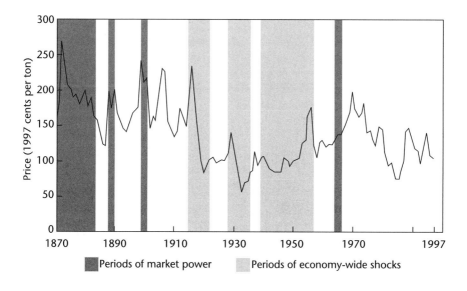

Periods of market power   Periods of economy-wide shocks

Figure 4-3. Real Copper Prices, with Occurrences of Cartels, Wars, Major Depressions, and Other Market Distortions, 1870–1997

Sources: Herfindahl 1959 and Mikesell 1979, as updated in Howie 2001.

commodities have fallen and the demand for mineral commodities has grown. This suggests that long-run prices may underestimate trends in scarcity. Thanks to OPEC and its effects on oil and other energy prices since the early 1970s, just the opposite may be true for the energy markets.

Some years ago, Herfindahl (1959) conducted an interesting study of copper prices and costs, and found that the effects of market power can be substantial. Carefully examining the period 1870 to 1957, he identifies the years during this period that were abnormal, in the sense that collusion, wars, or depression seriously distorted the copper price (see Figure 4-3). He also divides the years before World War I from those after it, because a revolutionary change in technology at around that time caused a one-time drop of 37 percent in real prices. Of particular interest for our purposes, he finds that the copper price deflated by the PPI declined during the 1870–1918 period by 5 percent a year when the abnormal years were excluded, in comparison with 4 percent a year when they were included. For the 1918–1957 period, the difference was much greater: Real prices increased by 0.2 percent a year when the abnormal years were excluded in comparison with 0.6 percent when they were included.

Herfindahl's work calls into question—at least for copper since 1918—the premise advanced above that a decline in market power over time has introduced a downward bias in our price measures of scarcity for the nonfuel mineral commodities. It also raises the possibility that long-run trends in the real prices of mineral commodities may contain breaks, or abrupt downward shifts, and thus fail to follow the smooth continuous trends so often assumed in studies (especially econometric studies) of mineral commodity prices. Finally, Herfindahl's study shows that systematic efforts to purge the distortions introduced by market power and other factors that cause prices to deviate from their market clearing values are possible.

Fifth, Slade uses the PPI to deflate the nominal prices of mineral commodities. Although this index is widely used, rarely is it justified beyond mentioning the need to eliminate the effects of inflation. There are, of course, other deflators one might use. As we have seen, Barnett and Morse (1963) find the prices of nonextractive goods most appropriate for their purposes. Nordhaus (1974) uses the cost of labor, and Krautkraemer (1998) the consumer price index (CPI). Another candidate is the gross domestic product (GDP) deflator.

Conceptually, the deflator used should depend on how we want to measure resource scarcity. This is done by considering the sacrifice, usually in terms of some basket of goods, that society has to give up to obtain an extra ton of copper or barrel of oil. If the desired sacrifice is a representative sample of all the goods and services (including those used by both consumers and producers) that make up the economy, then the GDP deflator is the most appropriate. If a representative sample of just consumer goods and services best measures the desired sacrifice, then the CPI should be used.

Either of these two baskets of goods would logically seem more appropriate than a basket of producer goods. Still, the PPI, which Slade and many others use, has the advantage that it is available during an extended period of time. In addition, there is little to suggest that the long-run trends in real mineral prices would be significantly altered if the GDP deflator or CPI were used instead (see Figure 4-4).[12]

A more serious shortcoming of the PPI and other commonly used deflators arises from their tendency to overestimate inflation, which is the result of their failure to account adequately for quality improvements in products, for the introduction of new products, and for the opportunities consumers have to substitute away from goods whose prices are rising (see Box 4-1). This would not be a problem for our purposes if the reported prices for mineral commodities were similarly biased, but this is clearly not the case. Appropriate adjustments for quality changes, new products, and user substitutions would not significantly alter the price for a particular grade of crude oil or for other mineral commodities. As a result, our long-run series of real mineral commodity prices underestimate the true trends (Svedberg and Tilton, forthcoming).

Figure 4-5 provides some indication of the potential magnitude of this bias. It shows the real price of crude oil during the 1870–1998 period, deflated first by the PPI, then by the PPI minus 0.75 percent a year, and finally by the PPI

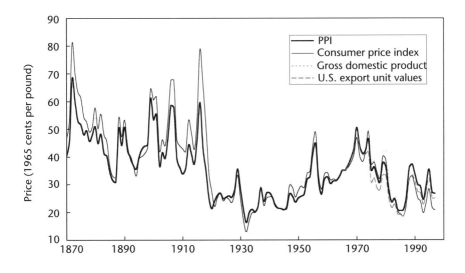

Figure 4-4. The Real Price of Copper Deflated by the Producer Price Index, Consumer Price Index, Gross Domestic Product Deflator, and U.S. Export Unit Values, 1870–1997

Sources: The copper price and producer price index deflator are from Potter and Christy 1962, Manthy 1978, and Howie 2001. The consumer price index deflator is the consumer price index for all urban consumers. It is from the *Historical Statistics of the United States to 1970*, available at the website http://www.lib.umich.edu/libhome/ Documents.center/historiccpi.html, for the years 1870 to 1912, and from http:// stats.bls.gov/ cpihome.htm, the website of the U.S. Bureau of Labor Statistics, for the years 1913 to 1997. The gross domestic product deflator is the NIPA-GDP Implicit Price Deflator. It is from the *Survey of Current Business, August 2000*, which is available from http:// www.bea.doc.gov/bea/dn/st-tabs.htm, the website of the U.S. Bureau of Economic Analysis, for the years 1929 to 1997. The U.S. Export Unit Values index indicates the price changes in the goods the United States exports. It is from the International Monetary Fund (monthly) for the years 1965 to 1997.

minus 1.25 percent a year. The price for petroleum properly adjusted for inflation could very well lie somewhere between the last two curves. If so, the long-run trend in real petroleum prices—which appears quite flat during the 1870–2000 period when deflated by the PPI—has clearly been rising. Comparable changes in the long-run trends for other mineral commodities occur when their prices are similarly adjusted, raising questions about the conclusions of Barnett and Morse as well as many other researchers regarding the stability of real prices for mineral commodities during the past century.

Box 4-1. Common Deflators Overestimate Inflation

For some time, economists and others have recognized that our common deflators overestimate inflation. For example, Hamilton (2001), using an indirect estimation procedure, has recently suggested that the CPI overestimated inflation by about 3 percent a year between 1974 and 1981 and by about 1 percent a year from 1981 to 1991.

Several years ago, a congressional advisory commission estimated that the U.S. CPI overestimates inflation by 1.1 percent a year (U.S. Senate, Committee on Finance 1966; Boskin and others 1998; Moulton and Moses 1997). Most of this bias (0.6 percent) is attributed to the introduction of new goods and improvements in the quality of existing goods, which the CPI often ignores. The rest reflects the failure of the consumer price index to account properly for consumer substitutions in response to price changes (0.4 percent) and for discount stores and other improvements in retailing (0.1 percent).

More recently, a study sponsored by the National Research Council (Schultze and Mackie 2002) examines a number of conceptual and empirical issues regarding measuring the CPI, raising some questions about the specific figures cited by the congressional advisory commission. In any case, these exact percentages presumably do not apply to the PPI. Nevertheless, there is little doubt that the PPI also overestimates the rate of inflation.

The above reservations about the Slade model are all legitimate concerns. What is less clear is how they, particularly when combined, affect her findings and the implications for the long-run availability of mineral commodities. We will revisit this issue at the end of this chapter.

User Costs

Our third economic measure of long-run trends in resource availability is user costs. As Chapters 2 and 3 pointed out, user costs are the present value of the future profits that a mine loses as a result of increasing current output by one unit. Moreover, it is important to stress that the relevant mine is the marginal producer, as the current market price just covers its extraction costs plus user costs. Intramarginal mines enjoy relatively low extraction costs, thanks to particularly good ore or other considerations. So expanding current output by one unit causes intramarginal mines to suffer a greater loss of future profits than marginal producers, but this loss reflects both user costs and the Ricardian rent associated with the quality of reserves (see Figure 3-2).

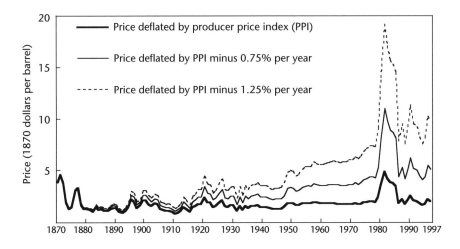

Figure 4-5. The Real Price of Petroleum Deflated by the Producer Price Index (PPI), PPI Minus 0.75 Percent a Year, and PPI Minus 1.25 Percent a Year, 1870–1997

Sources: For oil prices, deflated by the PPI: Potter and Christy 1962, Manthy 1978, Slade 1982, as updated in Howie 2001.

Although Hotelling, Slade, and others anticipate on the basis of theory that user costs will rise over time at some fixed percentage rate, this result holds only under a fairly restrictive set of conditions, as Hotelling explicitly notes (see Chapter 2). For example, he assumes only one homogenous ore (hence no differences in grade or other characteristics) and no technological change. Relaxing either of these assumptions allows user costs to follow other trends, including a decline in the long run. Should the development of cheap solar power, for example, make the production of coal and natural gas uneconomic, the user costs associated with coal and natural gas production would fall to zero, because there would be no loss of future profits as a result of producing more today.

Thus, there is a need to measure trends in user costs. It is not surprising that marginal mines do not report (and probably are seldom aware of) the expected net present value of the loss in future profits they incur by increasing their output an additional unit today. This means indirect measures of user costs are necessary. Assuming resource markets are competitive and certain other conditions, user costs reflect the in situ value (the value in the ground before extraction) of the reserves that the marginal mine owns and is exploiting. This in turn, again under the proper conditions, approximates the costs of finding such reserves. As a result, three indirect methods exist for estimating long-run trends in user costs for mineral commodities: the difference between their market price and marginal costs of production, the in situ value of marginal reserves, and the expected exploration costs of finding new marginal reserves.

None of these measures is easy to estimate during long periods due to a dearth of data and other problems. As a result, published studies on user costs are far less numerous than those on mineral prices. Moreover, the studies that do exist come to different conclusions. A few (Fisher 1981; Stollery 1983; Sadorsky 1991) find evidence of increasing user costs. Halvorsen and Smith (1991) fail to find any significant trend. Others (Farrow 1985; Pesaran 1990; Lasserre and Ouellette 1991) conclude that user costs are falling.

Part of the explanation for this confusing state of affairs lies in differences among the studies. They use different methodologies, examine different sets of mineral commodities, and cover different time periods.

Probably of more importance, however, is the fact that user costs, though a fascinating intellectual construct, may well be of little or no significance in practice. As Kay and Mirrlees (1975) note, user costs are negligible when discounted back to the present for mineral commodities that are sufficiently abundant to last for a long time—50 to 100 years—which is the case for many mineral commodities. Cairns (1998, 20) reaches the same conclusion, in part on the basis of his attempt (Cairns 1982) to measure the user costs of Inco's nickel resources. Similarly, Adelman (1990) finds that the user costs for petroleum are negligible.[13]

The behavior of mine managers also suggests that user costs are for the most part insignificant. It is difficult, if not impossible, to find instances where mine managers have deliberately reduced profitable production on the grounds that the resulting increase in future profits, properly discounted, more than makes up for the loss in current profits. Indeed, it is rare to find mine managers who are even familiar with the concept of user costs.[14]

The uncertainty created by new technology and other unexpected developments may simply make user costs largely or entirely irrelevant in the real world. Radetzki (1992), for example, points out that Sweden benefited greatly from the exploitation of its iron ore deposits from the beginning of the twentieth century through the 1950s. However, the ability of these mines to compete, which was largely based on their close proximity to the steel industries of Europe, was undermined during the 1960s and 1970s by the technological revolution in the ocean transport of bulk commodities. Had Sweden decided to save these deposits in the hope of realizing even larger (discounted) profits in the future, the country would likely have reaped no benefits. The true user costs of mining Swedish iron ore in the first half of the twentieth century apparently were zero.

Other examples of once valuable resources becoming worthless as a result of new technology and other developments are easy to find. Despite the concerns of Jevons noted in chapter 2, the United Kingdom has not run out of coal. Its deposits, however, are for the most part worthless, as a result of the discovery and development of much cheaper coal deposits elsewhere and the subsequent development of alternative sources of energy. The invention of artificial fertilizer in Germany early in the twentieth century destroyed the thriving guano industry in Chile. Many potential asbestos and mercury mines have lost any value they might once have enjoyed as health and safety concerns have devastated the demand for these commodities.

If in practice, user costs are quite modest, as the preceding discussion suggests, then several implications follow. First, the conflicting findings noted above regarding trends in user costs are not surprising, because the trends in user costs, whether they are rising, falling, or stagnant, presumably are overwhelmed by other, more important factors. Second, known mineral resources in the ground have value largely because of their Ricardian rent, which arise thanks to their ability to produce mineral commodities at lower costs than at least some of the deposits being exploited. Marginal deposits with no Ricardian rent have very little value. Third, mining companies and others have little incentive to delay developing or to put "on ice" for the future undeveloped but potentially profitable mineral deposits.

Summary

The three economic measures just reviewed, as Chapter 3 pointed out, reflect different aspects or sources of scarcity. User costs focus on the availability of the resource in the ground. Marginal costs focus on the production process and its impact on availability. Prices reflect the combined effects of both trends in availability in situ and in production.

The available evidence on production costs indicates that the cost-reducing effects of new technology have more than offset the cost-increasing effects of the decline in the quality of the resources being exploited. As a result, production costs, at least when measured in terms of physical inputs, have fallen substantially for mineral commodities during the past century. Some of this decline, however, may merely reflect the failure of the available studies to take into account changes in input prices, and in particular the rise in real wages during the past century.

Historical trends in user costs and mineral commodity prices are even less clear. In the case of user costs, obtaining reliable data for an extended period is quite difficult. The few studies that are available come to different conclusions, most likely because user costs are quite modest in practice.

Although reliable data are not a problem for mineral prices, interpreting the trends is. Some studies see long-run price as stationary, and conclude growing scarcity is not a problem. Others find trends following a U-shaped curve over time, and conclude that scarcity is on the rise. To this, one must add the problems of identifying the appropriate price deflator and the uncertainties they introduce, and of estimating a trend that periodically changes in some unknown way.

Despite such difficulties, the available evidence does permit two general conclusions. First, during the past century, a period when the demand for mineral commodities has exploded and the world has consumed more mineral resources than during all of its previous history combined, the depletion of mineral resources has not produced serious scarcity problems. The consumption of most mineral commodities today is as high as it has ever been. Although long-run trends in mineral prices may be confusing, they have clearly not forced the world to curtail its mineral consumption. As Krautkraemer (1998, 2091) notes:

> Economic indicators of nonrenewable resource scarcity do not provide evidence that nonrenewable resources are becoming significantly more scarce. Instead, they suggest that other factors of nonrenewable supply, particularly the discovery of new deposits, technological progress in extraction technology, and the development of resource substitutes, have mitigated the scarcity effect of depleting existing deposits.

In short, the past 130 years have been quite benevolent from the perspective of mineral resource availability.

Second, history also strongly suggests that the long-run trends in mineral prices, and more generally in the availability of mineral commodities, are not fixed. Rather they shift from time to time in response to changes in the pace at which new technology is introduced, in the rate of world economic growth, and in the other underlying determinants of mineral supply and demand. This not only complicates the task of identifying the long-run trends that have prevailed in the past, but cautions against using those trends to predict the future. Because the trends have changed in the past, they presumably can do so as well in the future.

The lessons to be learned from the past, it seems, are nicely summarized by Neumayer (2000, 309) when he states:

> So far, the pessimists have been wrong in their predictions. But one thing is also clear: to conclude that there is no reason whatsoever to worry is tantamount to committing the same mistake the pessimists are often guilty of—that is the mistake of extrapolating past trends. The future is something inherently uncertain and it is humans' curse (or relief, if you like) not to know with certainty what the future will bring.

The past can be a bad guide into the future when circumstances are changing. That the alarmists have regularly and mistakenly cried "wolf!" does not a priori imply that the woods are safe.

Notes

1. See, for example, U.S. Bureau of Mines 1987 and Torries 1988, 1995.

2. For an exception, see Hall and Hall 1984.

3. The U.S. wholesale price index became the producer price index in 1978. To avoid confusion, this study refers to both by the current name, the producer price index, or by its abbreviation, PPI.

4. Potter and Christy (1962) provide price data for four energy commodities (petroleum, natural gas, bituminous coal, and anthracite coal), for 14 metals (iron ore, pig iron, steel, ferroalloys, ferromanganese, nickel, tungsten, copper, lead, zinc, bauxite, aluminum, tin, and magnesium), and for 14 nonmetals (dimension stone, crushed and broken stone, portland cement, lime, sand, gravel, clays, structural clay products, building brick, gypsum, phosphate rock, potash, sulfur, and fluorspar).

5. As noted above, Barnett and Morse (1963) measure production costs in terms of the physical inputs of labor and capital, which ignores the effect of changes in input prices, and in particular the sharp rise in real wages during the past century. This may explain much of the difference between the long-run trends in production costs and the long-run trends in real mineral prices that Barnett and Morse observe.

6. The disturbance term allows the price in any year t to deviate from its trend value.

7. The first is the Brown and Durbin cusum test, and the second is the Quandt log-likelihood ratio.

8. This possibility is also suggested by Pindyck (1978) and Heal (1981).

9. The results for the linear equation compared with those for the quadratic equation suggest that the latter more accurately reflects the true relationship between mineral prices and time. First, as was noted, all but one of the estimated parameters for the square of time variable in the quadratic equation are positive at the 90 percent probability level. If the true relationship between prices and time were linear, this parameter would be zero. Moreover, all of the estimated linear relationships considerably underestimate mineral prices toward the end of the period covered, which is not the case for the estimated quadratic relationships. It is interesting that the results for the linear equation provide much less support for the conclusion that mineral resources are experiencing increasing scarcity. Only 7 of the 11 estimated parameters on the time variable were positive, and only 4 of these had a probability level of 90 percent or higher.

10. These results pertain when Howie uses the econometric techniques employed by Slade. When he uses more modern time-series techniques, the aluminum price series is best represented by the linear trend rather than the inverse trend. In addition, the estimated coefficients for the time variables in the equations for lead and zinc in all three specifications (linear, quadratic, and inverse) are statistically insignificant, raising the possibility that lead and zinc prices follow a linear trend that is moving neither upward nor downward over time.

11. For studies of cartels in the mineral and energy industries, see Eckbo 1976 and Schmitz 1995.

12. We do know from our earlier discussion of Nordhaus 1974 that using the cost of labor makes a big difference. Because labor costs have risen much more than the costs of most goods and service, deflating by labor costs produces real mineral prices that distinctly trend downward over the long run. Deflating by the cost of labor is appropriate when one desires to measure the sacrifice in terms of how much labor (leisure) one can buy for the price of an additional unit of a mineral commodity. As was noted above, however, it suffers from the fact that improvements in the quality of labor are in part behind the rising costs of labor over time. In addition, it implies that the appropriate basket of goods for measuring the opportunity costs contains just one good, labor services.

13. He does, however, note that this could change. Without the collusive efforts of OPEC, he argues the price of oil would be lower and production higher. If this caused the costs of developing new reserves to rise, user costs would similarly increase.

14. As Cairns (1998) points out, however, mine managers may not be concerned with user costs because the optimal mine capacity automatically optimizes the value of reserves. Managers determine the present value of reserves by their choice of investment in productive capacity. Output is then determined by capacity.

References

Adelman, M.A. 1990. Mineral Depletion, with Special Reference to Petroleum. *Review of Economics and Statistics* 72(1): 1–10. This article is reprinted in *The Economics of Petroleum Supply: Papers by M.A. Adelman 1962–1993*, edited by M.A. Adelman (1993). Cambridge, MA: MIT Press, ch. 11.

Agbeyegbe, T.D. 1993. The Stochastic Behavior of Mineral Commodity Prices. In *Models, Methods, and Applications in Econometrics: Essays in Honor of A.R. Bergstrom*, edited by P.C.B. Phillips. Oxford: Blackwell Science, 339–352.

Ahrens, W.A., and V.R. Sharma. 1997. Trends in Natural Resource Commodity Prices: Deterministic or Stochastic? *Journal of Environmental Economics and Management* 33: 59–77.

Barnett, H.J. 1979. Scarcity and Growth Revisited. In *Scarcity and Growth Reconsidered*, edited by V.K. Smith. Baltimore, MD: Johns Hopkins University Press for Resources for the Future, 163–217.

Barnett, H.J., and C. Morse. 1963. *Scarcity and Growth*. Baltimore, MD: Johns Hopkins University Press for Resources for the Future.

Berck, P. 1995. Empirical Consequences of the Hotelling Principle. In *Handbook of Environmental Economics*, edited by D. Bromley. Oxford: Basil Blackwell, 202–221.

Berck, P., and M. Roberts. 1996. Natural Resource Prices: Will They Ever Turn Up? *Journal of Environmental Economics and Management* 31: 65–78.

Boskin, M.J., and others. 1998. Consumer Prices, the Consumer Price Index, and the Cost of Living. *Journal of Economic Perspectives* 12(1): 3–26.

Cairns, R.D. 1982. The Measurement of Resource Rents: An Application to Canadian Nickel. *Resources Policy* 8(2): 109–116.

———. 1998. Are Mineral Deposits Valuable? A Reconciliation of Theory and Practice. *Resources Policy* 24(1): 19–24.

Cleveland, C.J. 1991. Natural Resources Scarcity and Economic Growth Revisited: Economic and Biophysical Perspectives. In *Ecological Economics: The Science and Management of Sustainability*, edited by R. Costanza. New York: Columbia University Press, 289–317.

Eckbo, P.L. 1976. *The Future of World Oil*. Cambridge, MA: Ballinger.

Farrow, S. 1985. Testing the Efficiency of Extraction from a Stock Resource. *Journal of Political Economy* 93(3): 452–487.

Fisher, A.C. 1981. *Resource and Environmental Economics*. Cambridge: Cambridge University Press.

Hall, D.C., and J.V. Hall. 1984. Concepts and Measures of Natural Resource Scarcity with a Summary of Recent Trends. *Journal of Environmental Economics and Management* 11(4): 363–379.

Halvorsen, R., and T.R. Smith. 1991. A Test of the Theory of Exhaustible Resources. *Quarterly Journal of Economics* 106(1): 123–140.

Hamilton, B.W. 2001. Using Engel's Law to Estimate CPI Bias. *American Economic Review* 91(3): 619–630.

Heal, G. 1981. Scarcity, Efficiency and Disequilibrium in Resource Markets. *Scandinavian Journal of Economics* 83(2): 334–351.

Herfindahl, O.C. 1959. *Copper Costs and Prices*. Baltimore, MD: Johns Hopkins University Press for Resources for the Future.

Howie, P. 2001. *Long-Run Price Behavior of Nonrenewable Resources Using Time-Series Models*. Unpublished manuscript, Colorado School of Mines. Golden, CO.

International Monetary Fund (monthly). *International Financial Statistics*. Washington, DC: International Monetary Fund.

Johnson, M.H., and others. 1980. Natural Resource Scarcity: Empirical Evidence and Public Policy. *Journal of Environmental Economics and Management* 7(4): 256–271.

Kay, J.A., and J.A. Mirrlees. 1975. On Comparing Monopoly and Competition in Exhaustible Resource Exploitation. In *The Economics of Natural Resource Depletion*, edited by D.W. Pearce. London: Macmillan, 140–176.

Kendrick, J.W. 1961. *Productivity Trends in the United States Economy*. Princeton, NJ: Princeton University Press for the National Bureau of Economic Research.

Krautkraemer, J.A. 1998. Nonrenewable Resource Scarcity. *Journal of Economic Literature* 36: 2065–2107.

Lasserre, P., and P. Ouellette. 1991. The Measurement of Productivity and Scarcity Rents: The Case of Asbestos in Canada. *Journal of Econometrics* 48(3): 287–312.

Manthy, R.S. 1978. *Natural Resource Commodities: A Century of Statistics*. Baltimore, MD: Johns Hopkins University Press for Resources for the Future.

Mikesell, R.F. 1979. *The World Copper Industry*. Baltimore, MD: Johns Hopkins University Press for Resources for the Future.

Moulton, B.R., and K.E. Moses. 1997. Addressing the Quality Change Issue in the Consumer Price Index. *Brookings Papers on Economic Activity* (1): 304–366.

Nappi, C. 1988. Canada: An Expanding Industry. In *The World Aluminum Industry in a Changing Energy Era*, edited by M.J. Peck. Washington, DC: Resources for the Future, 175–221.

Neumayer, E. 2000. Scarce or Abundant? The Economics of Natural Resource Availability. *Journal of Economic Surveys* 14(3): 307–335.

Nordhaus, W.D. 1974. Resources as a Constraint on Growth. *American Economic Review* 64(2): 22–26.

Pesaran, M.H. 1990. An Econometric Analysis of Exploration and Extraction of Oil in the U.K. Continental Shelf. *Economic Journal* 100(401): 367–390.

Pindyck, R.S. 1978. The Optimal Exploration and Production of Nonrenewable Resources. *Journal of Political Economy* 86(5): 841–861.

———. 1999. The Long-Run Evolution of Energy Prices. *Energy Journal* 20(2): 1–27.

Potter, N., and F.T. Christy Jr. 1962. *Trends in Natural Resource Commodities: Statistics of Prices, Output, Consumption, Foreign Trade, and Employment in the United States, 1870–1957.* Baltimore, MD: Johns Hopkins University Press for Resources for the Future.

Radetzki, M. 1992. Economic Development and the Timing of Mineral Exploitation. In *Mineral Wealth and Economic Development,* edited by J.E. Tilton. Washington, DC: Resources for the Future, 39–57.

Rogers, C.D. 1992. Tin. In *Competitiveness of Metals: The Impact of Public Policy,* by M.J. Peck and others. London: Mining Journal Books, 242–265.

Sadorsky, P.A. 1991. Measuring Resource Scarcity in Non-Renewable Resources with an Application to Oil and Natural Gas in Alberta. *Applied Economics* 23(5): 975–84.

Schmitz, C. 1995. *Big Business in Mining and Petroleum.* Brookfield, VT: Ashgate.

Schultze, C., and C. Mackie (eds.). 2002. *At What Price? Conceptualizing and Measuring Cost-of-Living and Price Indexes.* Washington, DC: National Academy Press.

Slade, M.E. 1982. Trends in Natural-Resource Commodity Prices: An Analysis of the Time Domain. *Journal of Environmental Economics and Management* 9: 122–137.

———. 1988. Grade Selection under Uncertainty: Least Cost Last and Other Anomalies. *Journal of Environmental Economics and Management* 15: 189–205.

———. 1992. *Do Markets Underprice Natural-Resource Commodities?* Working Paper No. 962. Washington, DC: The World Bank.

Smith, V.K. 1979. Natural Resource Scarcity: A Statistical Analysis. *Review of Economics and Statistics* 61: 423–427.

Stollery, K.R. 1983. Mineral Depletion with Cost as the Extraction Limit: A Model Applied to the Behavior of Prices in the Nickel Industry. *Journal of Environmental Economics and Management* 10(2): 151–165.

Svedberg, P., and J.E. Tilton. Forthcoming. The Real, Real Price of Nonrenewable Resources: The Case of Copper.

Torries, T.F. 1988. Competitive Cost Analysis in the Mineral Industries. *Resources Policy* 14(3): 193–204.

———. 1995. Comparative Costs of Nickel Sulphides and Laterites. *Resources Policy* 21(3): 179–187.

U.S. Bureau of Mines. 1987. *An Appraisal of Minerals Availability for 34 Commodities.* Washington, DC: Government Printing Office.

U.S. Senate, Committee on Finance. 1996. *Final Report of the Advisory Commission to Study the Consumer Price Index.* Washington, DC: Government Printing Office.

Uri, N.D., and R. Boyd. 1995. Scarcity and Growth Revisited. *Environment and Planning A* 27: 1815–1832.

Chapter 5

The Uncertain Future

One of the important findings that emerges from the preceding chapter and its review of historical trends in resource availability is that extrapolations of past trends are not likely to provide reliable forecasts, whether these are projections of price, extraction costs, or user costs.[1] This, of course, is not a big surprise. The validity of such projections requires that trends in the important underlying factors governing the past—along with the complex mechanism by which they interact—remain unchanged during the forecast period. Or alternatively, if there are changes, they must completely offset each other so that their net effect is zero. On occasions, one of these conditions may hold, and such forecasts may turn out to be quite accurate. But this is more a matter of luck than of any true power to discern the future (see Box 5-1).

How then should we proceed? What, if anything, can we say about the future? An alternative approach, one more likely to produce useful insights than extrapolations of past trends, analyzes the important underlying determinants of long-run mineral supply and demand. It is this approach that we pursue here. Though the chapter begins with a brief look at the prospects for shortages during the next several decades, the focus is largely on the long term, a period that begins 50 years from now and stretches into the distant future.

The chapter introduces the cumulative long-run supply curve, a useful expository device for categorizing the important determinants of mineral availability. It also distinguishes between what we currently know and what is knowable, and it suggests that the two may be different.

Box 5-1. M. King Hubbert

M. King Hubbert (1962, 1969) was a geophysicist who believed that the production of petroleum and other mineral resources follows a bell-shaped curve, first rising to a peak and then declining along a symmetric path to zero. On the basis of this proposition, once the rate of increase in production begins to slow, one can extrapolate the curve over the top and down the other side. In this way, Hubbert predicted in the early 1960s that oil production would peak in the United States within a decade. When the actual turndown occurred in 1970, his views gained widespread attention and many adherents.

Hubbert curves and their use for forecasting still have a number of dedicated followers. Campbell (1997), for example, using variants of the Hubbert method, concludes that the ultimate recovery of conventional oil in the world is 1.8 trillion barrels. He defines ultimate recovery as cumulative production to date, current reserves, and the amount of oil yet to be found. More recently, again relying on Hubbert's approach, Deffeyes (2001, 158) argues that world oil production could peak as early as 2003, and that "there is nothing plausible that could postpone the peak until 2009."

The underlying logic of Hubbert's methodology rests on the physical characteristics of oil reservoirs. It ignores the influence of economic, political, and technological developments. Because higher prices, wars, and new exploration and extraction technologies can all alter the course of oil production over time, many analysts do not consider projections based on Hubbert curves highly reliable.

The Near Term

During the next 50 years, the world is unlikely to face serious shortages of mineral commodities as a result of resource depletion. Although global demand is expected to continue to grow, the reserves for almost all mineral commodities are sufficiently large to accommodate expected demand for at least several decades even at growth rates above those currently prevailing (see Table 3-1). We also know that reserves are not fixed, but are more appropriately thought of as working inventories. By exploration and other means, companies can and do add to reserves over time, and additions to global reserves have in the recent past occurred on a regular basis. This situation—coupled with the stable or falling production costs and prices for many mineral commodities during the past several decades—has produced a widespread consensus among the experts that the threat of mineral depletion is not an immediate concern.[2]

Of course, mineral commodity shortages may still arise. Mineral depletion, as Chapter 1 pointed out, is but one of several factors that can threaten availability. Others include wars, accidents, strikes, political instability, and cartels. Insufficient investment in new mines and processing facilities may occur when demand grows faster than anticipated. In addition, the markets for mineral commodities are known for their cyclical instabiiity, with shortages and high prices when the world economy is booming, and gluts and low prices when the world economy is depressed. In contrast to mineral depletion, the influence of these market disturbances tends to be temporary, often lasting no more than several years, and rarely more than a decade or two. Nevertheless, during the next 50 years, and probably far into the future, they can be counted on from time to time to cause temporary mineral commodity shortages.

The Long Term

Far less agreement exists among the experts regarding the long-run threat of mineral depletion. On one side of the ongoing debate are the pessimists, often scientists and engineers, who are convinced that the earth cannot forever support the world's demand for oil and other mineral resources.[3] On the other side are the optimists, often economists, who with equal conviction believe that the earth—with the help of market incentives, appropriate public policies, material substitution, recycling, and new technology—can satisfy the world's needs far into the future.[4]

Different Paradigms and Faith in Technology

Just why the experts remain so polarized after decades of discussion and debate is not entirely clear. Part of the explanation lies in the different paradigms that each school tends to employ (Tilton 1996). The pessimists, as Chapter 1 pointed out, see mineral resources as nonrenewable over any time horizon of relevance to the human race. So supply is a fixed stock that can only diminish with use. Moreover, many believe that an expanding population and rising per capita incomes are causing the demand for mineral commodities to grow rapidly, hastening the day when the world's mineral resources will be gone.

The optimists look at resource depletion in an entirely different way. They find the ultimate fixed-stock nature of nonrenewable resource supplies irrelevant, in part because the quantities of mineral resources contained in the earth's crust could last for millions—and in a number of cases even billions—of years at current rates of consumption (see Table 3-2). Moreover, many nonrenewable mineral commodities—all the metals, for example—are not destroyed when used. The quantity of these resources found in and on the earth's crust is as great today as they have ever been.[5] Moreover, the substitution of abundant and perhaps renewable resources seems quite promising over the long term, particularly for petroleum and other nonrenewable sources of energy.

Finally—and this is a point on which a growing number of pessimists agree—increasing extraction costs and rising prices would cut off demand long before all of a mineral commodity was completely extracted from the earth's crust. As a result, a growing consensus is emerging among the more informed members of both schools that the fixed-stock paradigm should be retired in favor of an alternative that focuses on the opportunity costs of finding and extracting mineral resources.

The opportunity-cost paradigm stresses the differences among ore bodies. The deposits that are easiest to find and cost least tend to be exploited first. Over time, the depletion of these deposits forces society to turn to deposits that are lower grade, more remote, and more difficult to process. This tends to push production costs and mineral commodity prices up, reflecting their growing scarcity. Indeed, if prices rise sufficiently, demand will fall to zero and production will cease—even though uneconomic mineral resources remain in the ground. Economic depletion occurs before physical depletion becomes an issue.

Under the opportunity-cost paradigm, however, growing scarcity is not inevitable, contrary to the indicators of physical stocks. While depletion is pushing costs up over time, new technology, the discovery of new low-cost ore bodies, and other developments are pushing them down. If new technology, new discoveries, and other cost-reducing developments offset the cost-increasing developments of depletion, scarcity may decline and mineral commodity costs and prices may fall. As Chapter 4 documented, this favorable situation actually prevailed for much of the past century.

The optimists realize that the past is not necessarily a good guide to the future, but they stress that a rise in mineral commodity prices unleashes a host of countervailing forces. In particular, higher prices strengthen the economic incentives to develop new cost-saving technology, to discover new deposits, to recycle obsolete mineral commodities, and to find less costly substitutes. Such self-correcting mechanisms, they believe, make the economy far more resilient to the threat of depletion than many suppose.

The optimists also point out that population growth alters the supply of, as well as the demand for, mineral commodities. Although having more people promotes the need for mineral commodities, which tends to accelerate depletion and to increase the upward pressure on costs and prices, more people also means more good minds to create the new technologies that will offset the cost-increasing effects of depletion. As a result, population growth is not all bad for resource availability, and may not be bad at all. Julian Simon (1981) in

The Ultimate Resource argues that only human ingenuity, the ultimate resource, limits economic growth and the welfare of society. It is interesting that this argument was to a certain extent anticipated by Vincent McKelvey, a geologist and former director of the U.S. Geological Survey. McKelvey (1972) contends that human welfare, or what he calls society's average level of living, rises with the consumption of raw materials (metals, nonmetals, water, soil minerals, etc.), with the consumption of all forms of energy, and with the use of all forms of ingenuity (including political, social, economic, and technical ingenuity). Conversely, it declines as the number of people who must share the total output produced increases.

The pessimists, however, are well aware that these forces, and in particular new technology, have in the past kept mineral costs and prices from rising. Their concern, however, is for the future. They see the demand for mineral commodities rising rapidly, and question the wisdom of assuming that market incentives and new technology can indefinitely keep mineral scarcity in check. New technology for them is a two-edged sword, to be viewed with some suspicion. While dispensing its largesse (e.g., lower-cost mineral commodities), new technology also creates serious problems (e.g., climate change).

As the debate between the optimists and the pessimists suggests, the long-run availability of mineral commodities largely depends on a race between the cost-reducing effects of new technology and the cost-increasing effects of resource depletion. Although new technology has successfully offset the adverse effects of depletion during the past century, the course of new technology in the future is impossible to predict. This means that no one knows for certain the future trends in resource availability. Indeed, one might even be tempted to conclude that they are unknowable. This, however, may be too pessimistic. To illustrate why, we introduce the cumulative supply curve for mineral commodities.

The Cumulative Supply Curve

The *cumulative supply curve* for mineral commodities shows how the total or cumulative supply of oil, lead, or any other mineral commodity varies over all time with its price. It differs from the traditional supply curve found in introductory economic textbooks, which shows the quantity of a good offered to the market at various prices during a specific time period, such as a month or year. Supply figures provided by the cumulative supply curve are stock variables. Those provided by the traditional supply curve are flow variables, because they can continue from one period to the next indefinitely.

The cumulative supply curve makes sense only for commodities produced from nonrenewable resources. For wheat, automobiles, and many other goods, including renewable resources,[6] cumulative supply is infinite above a price that covers current production costs. For copper and other mineral commodities, however, cumulative supply at a particular price is fixed by the available quantities of the resources from which the commodity can be profitably extracted.

Like the traditional supply curve, the cumulative supply curve assumes that technology and all other determinants of supply, aside from price, remain fixed at their current prevailing levels (or at some other specified levels). Exploration and new discoveries can take place, but both exploration technology and the understanding of the geological sciences are presumed to remain unchanged.

Because rising prices permit the exploitation of poorer quality, higher cost deposits, the slope of the cumulative supply is positive. The higher the price, the greater cumulative supply. However, as Figure 5-1 illustrates, a variety of different shapes with very different implications for resource availability are consistent with an upward-sloping curve. The gradually rising curve in Figure 5-1(a) favors future availability, as small increases in prices allow large increases in cumulative supply. According to this curve, over time, rising cumulative consumption will evoke at most only modest increases in the costs and prices of mineral commodities. In contrast, curves b and c shown reflect situations in which, at some point, increases in cumulative supply require the exploitation of much more costly deposits, which in turn precipitates a sharp jump in price.

The many factors causing resource availability to change over time fall into three groups. The first group determines the shape of the cumulative supply curve. It encompasses various geologic factors, such as the incidence and nature of mineral occurrences. The second group determines how rapidly society advances up the cumulative supply curve. It includes population, per capita income, and other factors that shape the cumulative demand for primary mineral commodity production. The third group includes changes in

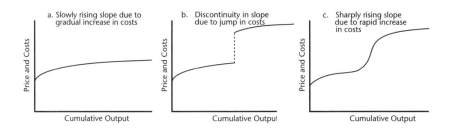

Figure 5-1. Illustrative Cumulative Supply Curves
Source: Tilton and Skinner 1987.

technology and input costs that cause the cumulative supply curve to shift over time.

The first two groups of factors determine the cost-increasing effects of depletion, whereas the third group reflects the cost-reducing effects of new technology. Whether mineral commodities become more or less available in the future, as we have seen, depends on the relative influence of these three groups on availability. What, if anything, do we know about their likely future evolution?

Geologic Factors

Whether or not the shape of the cumulative supply curve favors the future availability of mineral commodities depends on the number, size distribution, and nature of mineral occurrences. Some geologists, such as Lasky (1950a, 1950b), contend that as the grade declines—from 1.0 to 0.8 to 0.6 percent in the case of copper, for example—the amount of ore available increases by ever larger increments.[7] Such a favorable relationship implies a unimodal distribution between the recoverable quantities of copper and grade, similar to that portrayed in Figure 5-2(a).

Many other geologists—Singer (1977), for example—doubt that Mother Nature is so kind. They agree with Skinner (1976, 1979, 2001), who points out that the geochemical processes responsible for the formation of mineral deposits long ago, though still poorly understood, are unlikely to have created a unimodal relationship between grade (or more generally deposit quality) and the available quantities of any desired mineral commodity. Instead, Skinner argues that the relationship for many mineral commodities probably possesses two peaks, as portrayed in Figure 5-2(b), or even multiple peaks (see Box 5-2).

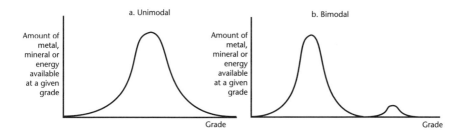

Figure 5-2. Two Possible Relationships between Ore Grade and the Metal, Mineral, or Energy Content of the Resource Base

Source: Skinner 1976.

Box 5-2. The Skinner Thesis

Skinner notes that the earth is composed of 92 chemical elements, which combine to form minerals, some of which society then extracts and processes into mineral commodities. Five of the 92 elements are so scarce they can for most purposes be ignored. The other 87 include nine abundant elements (oxygen, silicon, aluminum, iron, calcium, magnesium, sodium, potassium, and titanium), which together account for 99 percent of the weight of the earth's crust. The remaining elements, which are quite scarce, include copper, lead, zinc, tin, gold, and a number of other widely used metals.

The scarce elements, which are the focus of Skinner's analysis, are found in two types of mineralogical environments. In the first, they have replaced one of the more common elements in the widely available silicate minerals that make up most of the earth's crust. For example, the common mineral biotite often contains very small amounts of copper, zinc, nickel, and other scarce metals, whose atoms are sufficiently similar (in terms of size and electrical charges) to magnesium atoms to allow the former to replace the latter in the atomic structure of biotite. In this way, common rocks contain small amounts of all elements.

The second group of minerals is the result of various geochemical processes, most involving an aqueous fluid, that extract the scarce metals trapped in atomic substitution. The metals are then concentrated, transported, and finally precipitated from solution, forming quite different, nonsilicate minerals that contain copper or other scarce elements as major constituents. In this way, for example, the copper can be extracted from biotite, concentrated, and then precipitated as chalcopyrite or some other copper-bearing mineral.

Although the limits to atomic substitution vary with elements, physical and chemical conditions, and minerals, Skinner contends that typically they are reached when the scarce element rises to between 0.1 and 0.01 percent of the weight of the mineral. The limit constitutes a mineralogical barrier. Above the limit are found the separate (and scarce) ore minerals. Below the limit, the scarce metals are trapped in trace amounts within the atomic structure of common silicate minerals. Differences in the geochemical processes that create these two groups of minerals often produce a gap between the lowest grades of the ore minerals, which measures the percentage of copper or other metal that they contain, and the highest grade of the common minerals.

In this case, the grade–tonnage relationship is bimodal, as shown in Figure 5-2(b), rather than unimodal, as suggested by Lasky and as shown

The Skinner Thesis—*continued*

in Figure 5-2(a). Of course, if most of the copper, tin, and other scarce metals in the earth's crust were deposited in the ore minerals—that is the right-hand mode in Figure 5-2(b)—rather than the common minerals, this bimodal distribution would not be of great concern. According to Skinner (2001), however, the available geological evidence suggests just the opposite: Only 0.001 to 0.01 percent of the scarce metals in the earth's crust are available in the ore minerals; the rest are trapped in the atomic structure of the common minerals.

As the text points out, Skinner also contends that processing costs are likely to jump once the mineralogical barrier is crossed for reasons other than the decline in grade. The ore minerals, such as chalcopyrite in the case of copper, can be separated from other minerals recovered in the mining process using relatively inexpensive mechanical techniques (e.g., crushing and flotation). The result is a concentrate that may contain 30 percent or more of copper. The highly energy-intensive techniques required to liberate the copper trapped in the atomic structure of its ore mineral need only be applied to this concentrate. This is not the case when copper is extracted from silicates or other common minerals. Now energy-intensive separation techniques must be applied to all of the extracted material, which Skinner estimates increases the energy costs alone by a factor of 10 to 100.

The Skinner thesis, as he points out (Skinner 2001), does not apply to the energy minerals, such as oil, natural gas, and coal. Nor does it apply to the common metals, such as iron, aluminum, magnesium, and titanium. But it does apply to a large number of mineral commodities, including many important metals that society could not easily do without. The exclusion of the common metals has led Skinner and his fellow authors (Gordon and others 1987) to argue in a book entitled *A Second Iron Age Ahead?* that eventually the production of metals will shift toward iron and the other common metals, and away from the scarce metals.

Whereas the unimodal relationship favors a continuous cumulative supply curve with a decreasing slope over a wide range of quantities and prices, the bimodal curve is more troubling. It implies that the cumulative supply curve contains a discontinuity in its slope, as shown in Figure 5-1(b), or a steep jump in its slope, as shown in Figure 5-1(c), at the point where the high-grade deposits (which contain the ore minerals, some of which are currently being mined) are exhausted and much lower-grade deposits (which contain the common minerals that make up much of the earth's crust) must be brought into production.

Empirical studies of the relation between grade and tonnage do exist for a few mineral commodities (or, more correctly, by geologic deposit type).[8] However, as Singer and DeYoung (1980) and Skinner (2001) note, the available data for the most part come either from operating mines or from deposits that may not be economic at the present time but whose origins are similar to those of operating mines. So they provide little insight into how resource availability varies with grade for deposits whose geochemical origins differ from those of operating mines.[9] Because most of the world's supply of mineral commodities is found in such deposits, this is a problem. In addition, according to Harris and Skinner (1982), several biases in the available data may exaggerate the negative relationship between grade and tonnage. They raise the possibility that as grade declines the incremental additions in tons may not increase in quantity. So there is much we still need to know before we can be certain that the availability of mineral resources increases at an increasing rate as grade declines.

The nature of mineral deposits may also affect the shape of the cumulative supply curve. As depletion occurs, it may be necessary to bring entirely different types of deposits into production, which require a substantial increase in the energy and other inputs to process (Skinner 1976). For example, today the copper found in sulfide ores is concentrated by crushing and flotation before it is smelted and refined. Because smelting and refining are highly energy intensive, this substantially reduces production costs. Copper is also found in silicate resources, which are not amenable to concentration. Figure 5-3 indicates that the energy inputs needed for the highest-grade silicate ores, a type of common rock, could be as much as 10 to 100 times greater than for the lowest-grade sulfide ores. This could cause a sharp rise in processing costs, and a discontinuity or jump in the slope of the cumulative supply curve, should it eventually become necessary to extract copper from silicate minerals.

The jump in costs and the discontinuity in the cumulative supply curve, however, occurs only if there is not a substantial overlap of grades among sulfide and silicate ores. If the curve in Figure 5-3 for the silicate ores extends sufficiently to the right and downward, it may be possible to move from very low-grade sulfide ores to higher-grade silicate ores without a significant increase in energy or other costs. This fortuitous situation is known to exist for barium, lithium, nickel, and possibly copper (thanks to the copper found in seabed nodules). It is for this reason that one finds nickel currently being produced from both sulfide and silicate (laterite) deposits.

For other metals, however, crossing the mineralogical barrier may mean dramatic increases in costs. Although the implications for the long-run avail-

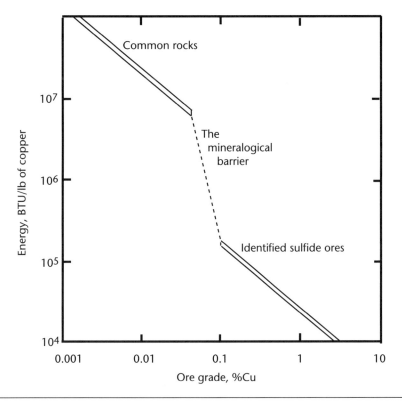

Figure 5-3. Energy Required per Pound of Copper from Sulfide Ore and Common Silicate Rock

Source: Skinner 1976.

ability of mineral commodities are obvious, they have not received a great deal of attention. Little economic incentive exists to analyze such potential problems until the need to use new types of mineral resources actually arises or at least is foreseen.

Demand for Primary Mineral Commodities

The second group of factors we need to examine governs the speed with which society moves up the cumulative supply curve. In this group are the four basic determinants of primary-mineral commodity demand: population, real per capita income, intensity of use, and secondary production (see Box 5-3).

Starting with *population*, let us examine each of these four variables. World population for centuries, even millennia, was both stable and small. As Figure 5-4 shows, it began to grow at an accelerating rate in the eighteenth century and exploded from 1.7 to 6.1 billion people during the twentieth century.

Box 5-3. Determinants of Total Demand for Primary-Mineral Commodities

Population, per capita income, and intensity of use determine the total demand—both primary and secondary demand—for a mineral commodity. Indeed, as equation 1 shows, an identity relates the product of these variables to total demand. This follows from the fact that by definition per capita income is total income (Y) divided by population (Pop), and intensity of use is the quantity of a mineral commodity demanded or consumed (Q) divided by income (Y). Therefore:

Total demand = (population) (per capita income) (intensity of use),

$$\text{or} \qquad\qquad\qquad 1$$
$$Q = Pop \times (Y/Pop) \times (Q/Y)$$

Subtracting secondary production (i.e., production from recycled scrap) from total demand leaves the demand for primary production. The latter summed from the present to any particular year in the future gives the cumulative demand for the commodity over the intervening period, and hence how far up the cumulative supply curve society will advance.

However, by the end of the twentieth century, the rate of growth was slowing, and a stable world population at slightly above 9 billion people is anticipated by the middle of the twenty-first century (U.S. Census Bureau 2001b).

The decline in population growth has been most pronounced in industrial countries. Rising per capita income tends first to increase life expectancy, stimulating population growth. Eventually, however, as development proceeds, the birthrate declines, causing population growth to slow and finally cease. In some industrial countries, such as France, population is actually shrinking. In others, only immigration keeps the number of people from falling. In many developing countries, demographers expect population to follow the slowing trends found in industrial countries. As a result, the strong upward push on the demand for mineral commodities that population growth has exerted during the past century will certainly diminish and probably cease in the coming century.

Although demographers can forecast population over the next 50 to 100 years with some accuracy, projections further into the future are notoriously difficult. Government policies, political stability, pestilence, economic conditions, customs, and human preferences all will influence birthrates and death rates in the future, but just how is impossible to project with any degree of accuracy more than a century or so into the future.

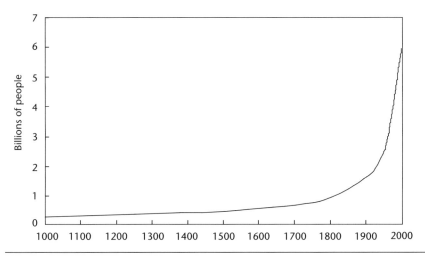

Figure 5-4. World Population, 1000–2000

Sources: U.S. Census Bureau 2001a, 2001b.

Per capita income is even more difficult to forecast into the distant future. Economists are still striving to understand fully why some countries have developed rapidly during the past century, while many millions of people have remained at or near subsistence poverty in other countries. Social and political institutions, human capital, and open and competitive economies are all widely acknowledged as important. But why these and other favorable conditions arise in some countries and not others, and at certain times but not others, still challenges the experts.

Clearly, if it is difficult to explain the past, it is even more of a problem to forecast when and where, and on what scale, economic development (as reflected by growth in per capita income) will take place in the future. We simply have little or no idea what the average per capita income for the world will be a hundred years from now, let alone in the more distant future. Developing countries are striving to achieve living standards comparable to those in industrial countries. Industrial countries, in turn, hope to maintain the growth in per capita income they have experienced during the past century. Although these aspirations may or may not be achieved, it is certainly plausible that real per capita income 50 years or more from now could be far above its current level.

Intensity of use reflects the consumption of a mineral commodity, usually measured in physical units, such as barrels of oil or tons of steel, divided by global gross domestic product (GDP), measured in dollars or some other monetary unit appropriately discounted over time for inflation.[10] It reflects the demand for mineral commodities per unit of income—the tons of copper consumed, for example, per billion dollars of GDP.

Some years ago, the International Iron and Steel Institute (1972) and Malenbaum (1973, 1978) advanced the hypothesis that the intensity of use for a mineral commodity depends on economic development as reflected by per capita income. Specifically, they argued that very poor countries with little or no development devote most of their efforts to subsistence agriculture and other activities that require minimal use of mineral commodities. Thus, their intensity of mineral use is low. As development takes place, however, their efforts shift to building homes, roads, schools, and hospitals. They begin to construct railroads and steel plants, and to consume first bicycles and then automobiles. Such activities push their intensity of mineral use upward. At some point, however, most of these needs are satisfied, and further development leads to another shift in preferences, this time toward education, medical care, and other services that are less mineral intensive.

For these reasons, the intensity-of-use hypothesis anticipates an inverted U-shaped relationship, such as that shown by curve C_1 in Figure 5-5, between per capita income and the intensity of use for mineral commodities. This hypothesis has over the years been used as a simple technique for forecasting the future consumption of mineral commodities, but with only partial success. For this and other reasons, it has received considerable criticism. Still, the basic idea

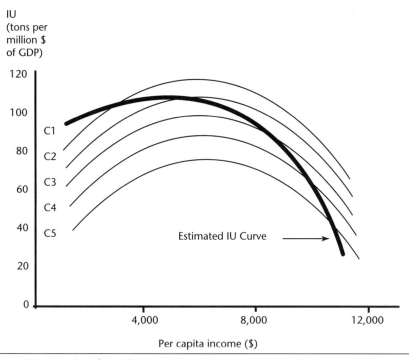

Figure 5-5. Intensity-of-Use Curves

that the intensity of mineral use depends on economic development and the changes in consumer preferences it produces seems quite plausible.

Other factors influence intensity of use as well. Government policies (e.g., increased public funding for defense or education), the introduction of new goods and services (e.g., computers and mobile telephones), shifts in demographics (e.g., a rise in the retired population), and other considerations (e.g., the decline in oil prices during the 1980s and 1990s that encouraged the demand for sport utility vehicles and small trucks) can along with changes in economic development produce shifts in consumer preferences. Such changes alter the mix of goods and services produced by the economy—what is called the product composition of income.

In addition, intensity of use may shift over time as a result of changes in the mineral commodities used to produce particular goods or services—what is called the material composition of products. These changes are largely driven by material substitution and resource-saving new technology. For example, the substitution of plastic beverage containers for aluminum cans increases the intensity of use of plastic and reduces the intensity of use of aluminum. Moreover, thanks to new technologies, we now make aluminum beverage cans with far thinner sheets and consequently less metal.

Because many factors affect intensity of use in addition to per capita income and economic development, the inverted U-shaped curve connecting intensity of use with per capita income is not stable, but rather shifts in response to changes in these other factors. Figure 5-5 portrays the intensity-of-use curve shifting downward over time from C_1 to C_2, to C_3, and so on. As a result, the intensities of mineral use that one actually observes over time as development occurs reflect various points on different intensity-of-use curves. These observed points trace out a hybrid curve, such as the heavy black curve shown in Figure 5-5.

The intensity-of-use curve can shift upward as well as downward. This occurred for aluminum, for example, when that material successfully displaced the tinplate beverage can in the 1970s and 1980s. For two reasons, however, the prevailing tendency at least for the widely used, traditional mineral commodities is for the curve to shift downward. First, resource-saving technology reduces but does not increase intensity of use. Bridges today can be built with far less steel than 50 years ago due to improved steels with far greater strength. New developments that increased the amount of steel required would not be advances and would not be introduced. Second, scientists and engineers are constantly developing new materials. During the past several decades, for example, many new plastics, ceramics, and composites have penetrated the market. For the traditional materials, this means that material substitution, though it may on occasions increase intensity of use, tends on balance to have the opposite effect as new materials capture part of their historical markets.

The same tendencies are found for energy minerals as well. New technology allows automobiles to go further on a gallon of gas, and the use of passive and active solar energy reduces the amount of natural gas and oil needed to heat homes and to provide hot water.

For these reasons, the intensity of mineral use is likely to decline in the future as rising per capita income alters consumer preferences and new technologies affect the use of mineral commodities.[11] This conclusion is reinforced by the available empirical studies (Tilton 1990; U.S. Energy Information Administration 2000), which show the intensity of use for important metals and energy resources falling over the long run.[12] Although this trend is likely to continue, forecasting the magnitude of the decline far into the future is not possible given the host of factors shaping intensity-of-use trends. Moreover, some determinants, such as the new technologies that will alter future mineral use, are simply impossible to anticipate.[13]

Recycling and *secondary production* cover the last of the four basic determinants of primary-mineral commodity demand. Normally, of course, we would consider secondary production as a source of supply, not as a determinant of demand. However, the cumulative supply curves shown in Figure 5-1 reflect only the production of primary-mineral commodities, not the production of both primary and secondary output. Whereas secondary production affects the amount of primary production, it does so by influencing the demand for, rather than the supply of, primary-mineral commodities.

Secondary production, though generally of little significance for energy-related minerals, is important for many metals. In the United States, for example, the recycling of old scrap currently accounts for respectively 12, 20, and 61 percent of the domestic consumption of copper, aluminum, and lead (U.S. Geological Survey 2001).

What then can we say about the future of recycling? First, secondary production is ultimately limited by the amount of scrap available for recycling. Because some scrap—lead in lead-based paint, for example—is prohibitively expensive to recycle, this means that secondary production by itself will almost certainly not meet the total future demand for mineral commodities. This would require a decline in demand sufficient to ensure that secondary production could provide all the needed output at costs below those of even the lowest-cost primary producer.

Second, and related to this first point, the faster the demand for a mineral commodity grows, the smaller the proportion of total consumption secondary production is likely to provide (Radetzki and Van Duyne 1985). This follows from the fact that the amount of old scrap available for recycling at any point in time depends on the amount of metal consumed in the past, often a decade or more earlier. So when demand is growing rapidly, only a small portion of current needs can be met by secondary production, even assuming all the available old scrap is recycled.

Third, secondary metal production is a close substitute for primary production, and so its future is closely tied to trends in primary metal markets. Although some scholars (Ayres 1997) contend that the role of secondary production must grow in the future, this conclusion rests on the assumption that primary resources will suffer a decline in availability. If depletion or other factors drive metal prices up, this will increase the demand and output of secondary copper. Alternatively, if new technology more than offsets the adverse effects of depletion, causing primary production costs to fall, secondary metal output will decline relative to primary production unless it can reduce its costs at an even greater rate (Tilton 1999).[14]

In short, the bleaker the prospects for primary production, the greater the likely role for recycling, and vice versa. This finding—though comforting in that it suggests that the beneficial impact of recycling increases with society's need—is not particularly helpful for the purpose at hand. It indicates that the amount of recycling in the future will depend on the availability of primary mineral commodities, which is exactly what we are trying to determine by assessing long-run trends in recycling and primary-mineral commodity demand.

This brief tour of the four basic determinants of the demand for primary-mineral commodities suggests that during the next century population growth will peak and then start to decline, real per capita income (barring a major catastrophe) will continue its upward climb, intensity of use will likely persist in its long-run decline, and recycling will account for a portion—perhaps a growing portion, perhaps a declining portion—of the world's consumption of major metals.

Although this is of some interest, we unfortunately have no clear picture of the net effect during the coming century of these conflicting influences, and thus how rapidly the world will move up the cumulative supply curve. Moreover, the view becomes even murkier as we venture further into the future.

Technology and Input Costs

Finally, we turn to the forces—changes in technology and input costs—that cause the cumulative supply curve to shift. Having seen that new technology on the demand side, which affects the use of mineral commodities, influences the speed with which society ascends the cumulative supply curve, we now focus on changes in technology that influence production costs and in turn the supply of mineral commodities.

Such new technology shifts the cumulative supply curve downward. If this were not the case, it would increase rather than reduce production costs, and so would not be adopted. Changes in input costs, however, can move the curve in either direction.

Labor, capital, energy, and materials are the crucial inputs for most mineral commodities. During the past century, the real cost of labor, at least in the United States and other industrial countries, has risen greatly, largely accounting for the dramatic improvements these countries have enjoyed in their standard of living. This has exerted upward pressure on the cumulative supply curve. Prices for the other three inputs have varied, at times rising and at other times declining.

Although these changes are important, new technology has dwarfed their impact on the cumulative supply curve. Barnett and Morse (1963), Simon (1981), and many of the other writers whose works were reviewed in earlier chapters stress the important role that new technology has played in reducing costs and increasing availability. In addition, the literature is filled with examples of important new technologies affecting mining and energy production in general as well as individual mineral commodities in particular.[15] Horizontal drilling for oil and gas, solvent-extraction electrowinning for copper, high pressure acid leach for nickel, longwall mining for coal, electric furnaces and minimills for steel, larger trucks and shovels, bigger and faster drills, satellite imagining for exploration, and computer controlled operations are but a few of the better-known new techniques that are making it easier and cheaper to produce mineral commodities.

It is, however, far easier to assess the impact of new technology in the past than to forecast its future effects. Indeed, projecting new technology is notoriously difficult, even over the near term. It is simply impossible to look 50 years and further into the future. We know the development and introduction of new technologies will continue, but we simply have no way to measure reliably their likely impact on production costs in the distant future.

Prospects for Resource Availability

Future trends in resource availability, we have seen, will depend largely on the outcome of the cost-increasing effects of depletion and the cost-reducing effects of new technology. On the positive side, the availability of mineral commodities is not likely to become a problem in the near term, during the next half-century.

In the long run, should mineral depletion cause shortages, they are likely to emerge gradually, perhaps over decades, as the real prices and costs of mineral commodities rise slowly but persistently. In this respect, shortages due to depletion are quite different from the abrupt but temporary shortages produced by wars, cartels, strikes, natural disasters, insufficient investment, and economic cycles. We also know that shortages caused by depletion, if they occur, would restrict the use of mineral commodities by raising their real prices, which in turn would increase secondary production. As a result, the world is not likely literally to run out of mineral commodities.

Moreover, even in the long run, depletion is not inevitable—at least on any time scale of relevance to humanity. Although past trends cannot be counted on to continue indefinitely, the future could conceivably be like the past, and enjoy growing rather than declining availability of mineral commodities.

Our efforts to assess long-run prospects on the basis of the fundamental factors influencing the supply and demand for mineral commodities came up wanting. Although providing some interesting insights, they encountered too many unknowns to make useful projections much beyond the next several decades.

So the central question remains unanswered. We simply do not know whether future trends in resource availability will foster or thwart the desires of people around the globe to improve their standard of living. Those who claim to have an answer to this question—and as we have seen, quite a few can be counted on both sides of the issue—explicitly or implicitly rest their claims on debatable assumptions, and in particular on assumptions about the future course of technology.

If the distant future is unknown, largely as a result of the impossibility of forecasting new technology, does this mean that the future is inherently unknowable? This query brings us back to the cumulative supply curve, and it raises two questions. Is it possible to assess the shape of this curve for individual mineral commodities? And if so, is it worthwhile?

The answer to the first question is probably yes. The necessary information, as pointed out above, entails geologic data on the number, nature, and size of mineral deposits that exist in the earth's crust. Already, considerable information exists for economic deposits (i.e., deposits that are currently profitable to exploit), which provides some knowledge about the shape of the lower end of the cumulative supply curve. Understandably, much less information is available for subeconomic deposits, because exploration companies and other private entities have few economic incentives to acquire knowledge about such deposits. Presumably, however, this information could be obtained if society were sufficiently concerned about future resource scarcity to foot the bill and thus provide the needed incentives. This would provide a clearer picture of the cumulative supply over a much wider range of ore grades and prices.

Of course, given the time value of money (see Box 2-1), obtaining information on deposits that are not now economic or close to being economic entails costs. As a result, public policies subsidizing the acquisition of this information are desirable only if the expected benefits derived from knowing more about the shape of the cumulative supply curve exceed these costs.

The answer to the second question is definitely yes. Mineral commodities whose cumulative supply curves rise gradually with no discontinuities or sharp upturns—and so are similar to the curve shown in Figure 5-1(a)—are less likely to suffer from significant scarcity even if their demand expands rapidly and technological change is ineffective in reducing their costs. In contrast, mineral commodities whose cumulative supply curves contain discontinuities or sharply rising segments are much more prone to scarcity.

In short, though the future availability of mineral commodities beyond the next 50 years is unknown, it may not be unknowable. Although the difficulties of forecasting technological change and its effects into the distant future make it impossible to determine how quickly society will move up the cumulative supply curve or how much the curve will shift downward, much can be learned about the shape of the curve. If society is concerned about mineral scarcity, investing in the geologic information that determines the shape of the cumulative supply curve would provide many useful insights on the threat that depletion poses in the long term.

Notes

1. This chapter is based on a lecture I have given over the years, often to audiences of geologists and earth scientists. It draws as well from Tilton and Skinner 1987 and Tilton 1991.

2. As the quote from Kesler in Chapter 2 indicates, this view, though widespread, is not universal.

3. Well-known members of the pessimistic school include Kesler (1994); Meadows and others (1972); Meadows and others (1992); Park (1968); and Youngquist (1997).

4. Julian L. Simon (1980, 1981) is probably the best known member of the optimistic school. Others include Adelman (1973, 1990), Beckerman (1995), and Lomborg (2001).

5. Many pessimists, it should be noted, recognize this point as well, as the following quote from Ayres (1993, 199) so clearly illustrates: "Resource exhaustion cannot mean physical disappearance of matter from the earth per se. It can mean, and is usually taken to mean, a change of form from desirable to undesirable. 'Useful' forms (or combinations) of elements, such as fossil fuels and metal ores, are being used up and converted into 'useless' (e.g., worn out) or even harmful forms or combinations (e.g., wastes and pollutants)."

6. This assumes, of course, that the exploitation of renewable resources does not exceed their regeneration capacity.

7. For an interesting analysis of Lasky's work, see DeYoung 1981.

8. Singer and others (1975), for example, analyze how the tonnage of ore varies with grade for the three different types of copper deposits—porphyry, massive sulfide, and strata-bound—that are the main sources of current copper production. For the porphyry and strata-bound deposits, they find no significant tendency for tonnage to increase as grade declines. A significant negative relation does exist between tonnage and grade for the massive sulfide deposits and for all of the deposits they examine when combined.

For both statistical and geological reasons, however, they caution against extrapolating these results, and concluding that very low-grade but large tonnage copper deposits exist. In particular, they stress that such deposits would probably have to be quite different from any of the three important types currently being exploited. In addition to the work on copper by Singer and others, see Foose and others 1980 on nickel and Harris 1984 on uranium and copper.

9. One exception, which does provide some support for the Skinner thesis, is Cox 1979.

10. Much of the discussion that follows on intensity of use is based on Radetzki and Tilton 1990 and the sources it cites.

11. For a recent and comprehensive review of the literature on the intensity of material use, which is more skeptical about the downward trend over the long run in intensity of use, see Cleveland and Ruth 1999.

12. It is interesting that the intensity of use for copper and for a few other metals—both for the United States and for the world as a whole—rose during the 1990s, bucking previous trends (Crowson 1996). Part of the explanation for this surprising development lies in the recent growth in demand for communication and electronic equipment. How long this upward trend will continue, however, is not clear.

13. Labson and Crompton (1993) go even further, concluding that past trends for metal intensity of use are of little use in making inferences about the future, because one cannot generally conclude that time-series data on intensity of use are stationary. Labson (1995), however, modifies this conclusion after taking into account the structural break in the intensity of use that Tilton (1989, 1990) and others contend occurred in the early 1970s.

14. Of course, public policies that require or subsidize recycling could ensure a bright future for secondary production even though primary production is cheaper. Chapter 7 examines the role of public policy in fostering recycling.

15. For a sample of such studies, see Bohi 1999 for petroleum, Darmstadter 1999 for coal, Manners 1971 for iron ore, Barnett and Crandall 1986 for steel, Tilton and Landsberg 1999 for copper, and National Research Council 1990 and 2002 for the mining industry in general.

References

Adelman, M.A. 1973. *The World Petroleum Market*. Baltimore, MD: Johns Hopkins University Press for Resources for the Future.

———. 1990. Mineral Depletion, with Special Reference to Petroleum. *Review of Economics and Statistics* 72(1): 1–10.

Ayres, R.U. 1993. Cowboys, Cornucopians, and Long-Run Sustainability. *Ecological Economics* 8:189–207.

———. 1997. *Metals Recycling: Economic and Environmental Implications*. Third ASM International Conference, Barcelona, Spain, ASM International.

Barnett, D.F., and R.W. Crandall. 1986. *Up From the Ashes: The Rise of the Steel Minimill in the United States*. Washington, DC: Brookings Institution.

Barnett, H.J., and C. Morse. 1963. *Scarcity and Growth*. Baltimore, MD: Johns Hopkins University for Resources for the Future.

Beckerman, W. 1995. *Small Is Stupid*. London: Duckworth.

Bohi, D.R. 1999. Technological Improvement in Petroleum Exploration and Development. In *Productivity in Natural Resource Industries*, edited by R.D. Simpson. Washington, DC: Resources for the Future, 73–108.

Campbell, C.J. 1997. *The Coming Oil Crisis*. Brentwood, U.K.: Multi-Science Publishing Company.

Cleveland, C.J., and M. Ruth. 1999. Indicators of Dematerialization and the Materials Intensity of Use. *Journal of Industrial Ecology* 2(3): 15–50.

Cox, D.P. 1979. The Distribution of Copper in Common Rocks and Ore Deposits. In *Copper in the Environment, Part 2*, edited by J.O. Nriagu. New York: Wiley and Sons, 19–42.

Crowson, P.C.F. 1996. Metals Demand and Economic Activity: Some Recent Conundra. In *1996 Proceedings of the Mineral Economics and Management Society Fifth Annual Professional Meeting*, edited by Henry N. McCarl. Montreal, Quebec: Mineral Economics and Management Society, 28–42.

Darmstadter, J. 1999. Innovation and Productivity in U.S. Coal Mining. In *Productivity in Natural Resource Industries*, edited by R.D. Simpson. Washington, DC: Resources for the Future, 35–72.

Deffeyes, K.S. 2001. *Hubbert's Peak: The Impending World Oil Shortage*. Princeton, NJ: Princeton University Press.

DeYoung Jr., J.H. 1981. The Lasky Cumulative Tonnage-Grade Relationship—A Reexamination. *Economic Geology* 76: 1067–1080.

Foose, M.P., and others. 1980. *The Distribution and Relationships of Grade and Tonnage Among Some Nickel Deposits*. U.S. Geological Survey Professional Paper 1160. Washington, DC: U.S. Geological Survey.

Gordon, R.B., and others. 1987. *Toward a New Iron Age? Quantitative Modeling of Resource Exhaustion*. Cambridge, MA: Harvard University Press.

Harris, D.P. 1984. *Mineral Endowment, Resources, and Potential Supply: Theory, Methods for Appraisal, and Case Studies*. Oxford: Oxford University Press.

Harris, D.P., and B.J. Skinner. 1982. The Assessment of Long-Term Supplies of Minerals. In *Explorations in Natural Resource Economics*, edited by V.K. Smith and J.V. Krutilla. Baltimore, MD: Johns Hopkins University Press for Resources for the Future, 247–326.

Hubbert, M.K. 1962. *Energy Resources: A Report to the Committee on Natural Resources*. National Academy of Science Publication 1000D. Washington, DC: National Academy Press.

Hubbert, M.K. 1969. Energy Resources. In *Resources and Man*, edited by P. Cloud. San Francisco: W.H. Freeman, 157–239.

International Iron and Steel Institute. 1972. *Projection 85: World Steel Demand*. Brussels: International Iron and Steel Institute.

Kesler, S.E. 1994. *Mineral Resources, Economics and the Environment*. New York: Macmillan.

Labson, B.S. 1995. Stochastic Trends and Structural Breaks in the Intensity of Metals Use. *Journal of Environmental Economics and Management* 29: S34–S42.

Labson, B.S., and P.L. Crompton. 1993. Common Trends in Economic Activity and Metals Demand: Cointegration and the Intensity of Use Debate. *Journal of Environmental Economics and Management* 25: 147–161.

Lasky, S.G. 1950a. Mineral-Resource Appraisal by the U.S. Geological Survey. *Colorado School of Mines Quarterly* 45(1A): 1–27.

———. 1950b. How Tonnage and Grade Relations Help Predict Ore Reserves. *Engineering and Mining Journal* 151(4): 81–85.

Lomborg, B. 2001. *The Skeptical Environmentalist.* Cambridge: Cambridge University Press.

Malenbaum, W. 1973. *Material Requirements in the United States and Abroad in the Year 2000: A Research Project Prepared for the National Commission on Materials Policy.* Philadelphia: University of Pennsylvania.

Malenbaum, W. 1978. *World Demand for Raw Materials in 1985 and 2000.* New York: McGraw-Hill.

Manners, G. 1971. *The Changing World Market for Iron Ore, 1950–1980.* Baltimore, MD: Johns Hopkins University Press for Resources for the Future.

McKelvey, V.E. 1973. Mineral Resource Estimates and Public Policy. In *United States Mineral Resources*, Geological Survey Professional Paper 820, edited by D.A. Brobst and W.P. Pratt. Washington, DC: Government Printing Office, 9–19. This article also appears in *American Scientist* 60: 32–40.

Meadows, D.H., and others. 1972. *The Limits to Growth.* New York: Universe Books.

———. 1992. *Beyond the Limits.* Post Mills, VT: Chelsea Green Publishing.

National Research Council. 1990. *Competitiveness of the U.S. Minerals and Metals Industry.* Washington, DC: National Academy Press.

———. 2001. *Evolutionary and Revolutionary Technologies for Mining.* Washington, DC: National Academy Press.

Park Jr., C.F. 1968. *Affluence in Jeopardy: Minerals and the Political Economy.* San Francisco: Freeman, Cooper and Company.

Radetzki, M., and C. Van Duyne. 1985. The Demand for Scrap and Primary Metal Ores after a Decline in Secular Growth. *Canadian Journal of Economics* 18(2): 435–449.

Radetzki, M., and J.E. Tilton. 1990. Conceptual and Methodological Issues. In *World Metal Demand: Trends and Prospects*, edited by J.E. Tilton. Washington, DC: Resources for the Future.

Simon, J.L. 1980. Resources, Population, Environment: An Oversupply of False Bad News. *Science* 208: 1431–1437.

———. 1981. *The Ultimate Resource.* Princeton, NJ: Princeton University Press.

Simpson, R.D. 1999. *Productivity in Natural Resource Industries.* Washington, DC: Resources for the Future.

Singer, D.A. 1977. Long-Term Adequacy of Metal Resources. *Resources Policy* 3(2): 127–133.

Singer, D.A., and J.H. DeYoung Jr. 1980. What Can Grade-Tonnage Relations Really Tell Us? *Resources Minerales, Memoire du BRGM no. 106.*

Singer, D.A., and others. 1975. Grade and Tonnage Relationship among Copper Deposits. *Geology and Resources of Copper Deposits, Geological Survey Professional Paper 907-A.* Washington, DC: Government Printing Office for the U.S. Geological Survey.

Skinner, B.J. 1976. A Second Iron Age ahead? *American Scientist* 64: 158–169.

———. 1979. Earth Resources. *Proceedings of the National Academy of Sciences* 76(9): 4212–4217.

———. 2001. *Exploring the Resource Base.* Unpublished notes for a presentation to the Conference on Depletion and the Long-Run Availability of Mineral Commodities held in Washington, DC, April 22. New Haven, CT: Department of Geology and Geophysics, Yale University.

Tilton, J.E. 1989. The New View of Minerals and Economic Growth. *Economic Record* 65(190): 265–278

———. 1990. *World Metal Demand: Trends and Prospects*. Washington, DC: Resources for the Future.

———. 1991. The Changing View of Resource Availability. *Economic Geology* (Monograph 8): 133–138.

———. 1996. Exhaustible Resources and Sustainable Development: Two Different Paradigms. *Resources Policy* 22(1 and 2): 91–97.

———. 1999. The Future of Recycling. *Resources Policy* 25: 197–204.

Tilton, J.E., and H.H. Landsberg. 1999. Innovation, Productivity Growth, and the Survival of the U.S. Copper Industry. In *Productivity in Natural Resource Industries*, edited by R.D. Simpson. Washington, DC: Resources for the Future, 109–139.

Tilton, J.E., and B.J. Skinner. 1987. The Meaning of Resources. In *Resources and World Development*, edited by D.J. McLaren and B.J. Skinner. New York: John Wiley & Sons, 13–27.

U.S. Census Bureau. 2001a. Historical Estimates of World Population. http://www.census.gov/ipc/www/worldhis.html.

———. 2001b. World Population Information. http://www.census.gov/ipc/www/world.html.

U.S. Energy Information Administration. 2000. *Annual Energy Outlook 2001 With Projections to 2020*. Washington, DC: Government Printing Office.

U.S. Geological Survey. 2001. *Mineral Commodity Summaries 2001*. Washington, DC: Government Printing Office.

Youngquist, W. 1997. *GeoDestinies*. Portland, OR: National Book.

Chapter 6

The Environment and Social Costs

As Chapter 2 pointed out, the 1990s witnessed a shift in the debate over the long-run availability of mineral commodities. Fears that the environmental and other social costs incurred in the extraction, processing, and use of mineral commodities might severely constrain their future availability pushed aside the more traditional concerns about mineral depletion. Even if new technology allows the exploitation of poorer deposits without any significant increase in reported prices, it is argued that the environmental damage inflicted on society, along with the other social costs that the producer and consumer do not pay, may soon preclude the widespread use of mineral commodities.

Social costs cover all the costs associated with a particular activity. They include those costs for which the producing firm and in turn the consumer pay, such as the costs of labor, capital, and materials. These are called *internalized* (or *private*) costs, because the firm or party that uses these resources pays for them.

Social costs also include any external costs, or what are often referred to as simply *externalities*. These are costs that are borne by members of society other than the firm and the consumers who cause them. Automobile owners, for example, generate external costs in the form of pollution, noise, and congestion when they drive. When fossil fuel combustion at power stations spews particulates and other pollutants into the air, unless the firm is charged or fined, it and ultimately consumers do not pay all the costs of power generation. Some are inflicted on people who live downwind from the power plant.

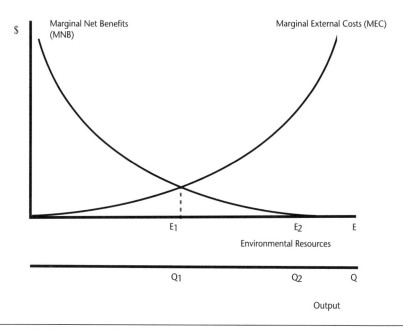

Figure 6-1. The Optimal Use of Environmental Resources

[a]The MNB curve indicates how the marginal net benefit to society from using an additional unit of an environmental resource (the deforestation of one more hectare) varies as the use of the environmental resource increases. This benefit reflects the additional profits the mining company earns on the extra iron ore mined.

[b]The MEC curve indicates how the marginal external costs—the environmental and other social costs that the mining company does not pay—from using an additional unit of an environmental resource (the deforestation of one more hectare) varies as the use of the environmental resource increases.

Externalities create problems. Society in effect subsidizes goods with external costs, because their market price does not reflect their full costs of production. This results in greater production than is optimal, in the sense that the costs to society of the last units of output exceed their benefits. Producers, moreover, have no incentive to conserve on environmental and other resources for which they do not pay. So these valuable resources are overused (see Figure 6-1 and Box 6-1).

In addition, for our purposes, external costs may mean that reported real costs and prices, such as those examined in Chapter 4, may no longer be reliable indicators of mineral resource availability, for two reasons. First, the exclusion of external costs means that the full social costs of mineral commodities (and in turn the basket of goods and services that society must give

Box 6-1. Iron Ore Mining in the Amazon

Figure 6-1 illustrates the distortions introduced by externalities, and it shows the optimal use of environmental resources from the perspective of society. The horizontal axis reflects the consumption of environmental resources, or alternatively the amount of environmental damage along with any other social costs incurred though the consumption of the resource (E). In practice, these costs may be measured by an appropriate proxy. Mendonça (1998) and Mendonça and Tilton (2000), for example, use the number of hectares deforested as a rough proxy for the environmental damage arising from iron ore mining in the Amazon region. If we assume that the use of environmental resources (deforestation) rises in direct proportion with output (iron ore production), the horizontal axis also reflects the output (Q) of the good causing the damage to the environment. When this is the case, a second line showing output (Q) can be drawn beneath the horizontal axis (E). The vertical axis measures the benefits and costs associated with using the environmental resource, measured in dollars or some other currency.

The marginal net benefit (MNB) curve shows the additional or marginal net benefit derived from using one more unit of the environmental resource (the deforestation of one more hectare). This in turn depends on the additional benefits that society realizes (from the additional iron ore that can be mined) as reflected in the extra profits the mining company earns as a result. Because profits per unit of output tend to fall as output increases, the curve slopes downward. The marginal external cost (MEC) curve shows the additional or marginal external costs—the environmental and other social costs that society but not the mining companies must bear—as a result of using one more unit of the environmental resource (again, for example, from the deforestation of one more hectare). Because the unit value of the remaining environmental resource is likely to rise as its supply declines, this curve slopes upward.

For society, the aggregate net benefits from mining in the Amazon are maximized when the additional costs of using one more hectare of land to produce iron ore just equal the additional benefits. This occurs where the two curves cross at a mine output of Q_1 and land deforestation at E_1. In this situation, some use of the environment—that is, some environmental damage—is desirable. Of course, this need not be the case. In some instances, the curve MEC may lie above the curve MNB across all levels of output and environmental resource use. This means that the social costs of production exceed the social benefits for all outputs, and

Iron Ore Mining in the Amazon—*continued*

so any production would on balance detract from, rather than add to, the well-being of society as a whole.

In either case, however, the mining company has an incentive to continue to produce until the MNB curve reaches zero, because it does not pay the environmental costs that the curve MEC reflects. Without some sort of government intervention, it will continue to produce and create environmental damage until output reaches Q_2 and environmental resource use E_2. The result is both too much output and too much pollution.

As the text notes, public policy can correct this situation either by regulating the mining industry and requiring it to produce at Q_1 using E_1 of environmental resources, or by imposing a tax of $0C$ dollars on each unit of environmental resource used or output of iron ore produced. If the tax is placed on the use of environmental resources rather than output, firms have an incentive to find new technologies and other ways of reducing the environmental resources required per unit of output. This stretches out the horizontal axis showing the output of the mineral commodities and also shifts the MNB curve outward, because any given amount of environmental resource can now accommodate a larger output.

For this and other reasons, the assumption that the use of environmental resources rises in direct proportion with output may in practice not hold. In this case, the optimal use of environmental resources is still determined by the intersection of the MNB and MEC curves, where the marginal net benefit of using one more unit of the environmental resources just equals the marginal external cost. The relationship between output and the use of environmental resources, however, no longer is linear, as is implied in Figure 6-1.

up to get an additional unit of any mineral commodity) is higher, perhaps far higher, than indicated by the available data on real costs and prices.

Second, when the external costs associated with mineral production change over time at a different pace than the internal costs, biases are introduced in the indicated trends in availability. For example, when the costs incurred by mining companies and the prices they charge are stable but their external costs are rising, the recorded costs and prices portray overly favorable trends in availability.[1] And turning from the past to the future, if environmental and other social costs are expected to rise rapidly, this could change the anticipated cumulative supply curve from one with a gradually increasing slope, when only internalized costs are considered, to one with a much steeper slope (see Figure 5-1), with all the unfavorable implications for the future availability of mineral commodities this implies.

The remedy most policy analysts recommend for the problems created by environmental and other external costs is for the government to limit output or environmental damage to its optimal levels. Because output is desirable but environmental damage is undesirable, restricting environmental damage rather than output has the advantage of encouraging mining companies to increase output (the good) to the extent they can and still limit their environmental damage (the bad) to its socially optimum level.

The government might, for example, impose regulations on mining companies requiring that their operations meet certain water or air pollution standards. An alternative is for the government to impose a tax on companies, often referred to as a *Pigovian tax*, after Arthur Pigou, the British economist, who first recommended this solution to the problem of externalities. Placing just the right amount of tax, for example, on environmental damage encourages producers to restrict their output and to reduce their environmental damage to the desired level. Again, a tax on environmental damage is preferable, because it is environmental damage not production that society wants to discourage.

Yet another possibility is to privatize the property rights for environmental assets and create markets with tradable permits. For example, the U.S. government under its Acid Rain Program—what Stavins (1998) calls the Grand Policy Experiment—has effectively given to producers the right to emit 8.9 million tons of sulfur dioxide annually (Ellerman 1999).[2] Of course, producers were using these environmental assets before they actually owned them. Ownership, however, led to a number of important developments. Firms now can buy and sell these assets, which provides an additional incentive to use them as efficiently as possible.[3] The role of the government as regulator has been dramatically reduced and altered. Overall, the program appears to have produced substantial benefits for both the environment and the economy.

Historically, governments have relied primarily on *command-and-control regulations*, which directly govern the behavior of firms and consumers. Controls that require firms to use a particular technology, such as scrubbers or catalytic converters, are examples of command-and-control regulations. So too are limits on the maximum amount of pollutants that firms can emit into the environment during a given time period. The past several decades, however, have seen growing support for measures, such as taxes on emissions and tradable permit schemes, that affect behavior indirectly by altering the economic incentives confronting polluters.

By forcing companies to pay for the environmental resources they consume, governments encourage companies to strive just as hard to reduce their environmental damage as to conserve on the labor, capital, and other inputs they employ. This is a big advantage, because over time it permits more production with less pollution. In addition, economic incentives encourage companies—those engaged in mineral production, their suppliers, and others as well—to develop new technologies that reduce the environmental damage associated with mining. Finally, the prices of mineral commodities more closely reflect the full costs of production—and hence their true scarcity value.

It is even possible that the threat to the long-run availability of mineral commodities due to environmental and other social costs could be mitigated or completely eliminated by forcing producers and consumers to pay for these costs. Once this is done, new technology should reduce the erstwhile external costs associated with mining and mineral processing, just as it has reduced the labor, capital, and other internalized costs of resource production in the past.

For this to happen, however, public policymakers need to have the ability and the will to force firms to pay the environmental and other social costs associated with their production. Then, once these costs are fully internalized, firms must possess the capability to generate the requisite technologies. The rest of this chapter examines these two necessary conditions, starting with the second, because the prospects for its fulfillment seem more propitious.

Technology and Environmental Costs

A century ago—even 50 years ago—mineral-producing firms faced few environmental restrictions. The environment was largely viewed as a free good, for firms and others to use as they wished. As a result, there was little or no incentive to reduce environmental costs. Sulfur dioxide, particulates, and other pollutants from energy combustion were pumped into the air. Other wastes from mining were dumped on land or into nearby streams. Mines were abandoned with little or no reclamation.

This situation has changed greatly during the past several decades. The environment has become more valuable as the economy has expanded, and society has become richer. Governments around the world have imposed regulations and other controls on mineral producers and other firms. One interesting by-product of this development is the accumulating evidence indicating that mineral-producing firms as well as other enterprises can substantially reduce their environmental costs per unit of output when they have the incentives to do so. Environmental costs, it appears, are just as amenable to the cost-reducing effects of new technology as capital and labor costs—perhaps even more so at the present time because efforts to reduce environmental costs in the mining sector have been so modest until recently.

A comprehensive review of this evidence for the mineral sector is to our knowledge not yet available, and in any case is not necessary here. Several examples should suffice. A particularly interesting case is the lead industry in the United States. Figure 6-2 provides an interesting picture of the sources, uses, and ultimate fates or disposition for this commodity, first for 1970 and then for the years 1993–1994. While consumption grew by about 15 percent during this period, primary domestic production and net imports declined as recycling and secondary production more than doubled. Despite rising consumption, lead discarded back into the environment—including the lead in paint, gasoline, and other dissipated uses—fell by more than 50 percent. Government policies that regulated the recycling of motor vehicle batteries and that curtailed or eliminated for health reasons the use of lead in paints and gasoline deserve most of the credit for these favorable developments.

The aluminum industry in Canada provides another example. As Figure 6-3 shows, it managed between 1972 and 1995 to reduce its emissions of particulates, fluoride, and polycyclic aromatic hydrocarbons (PAHs)[4] by 67, 69, and 86 percent respectively, all while more than doubling its output.

Recently, Alcoa has applied for a patent on a new process that would use fuel cells to generate the electricity to smelt alumina into aluminum. Although commercial development may take a decade or longer, analysts (Van Leeuwen 2000) believe that the new technology could reduce the amount of carbon dioxide generated per pound of aluminum from nearly 17 pounds for the conventional technology using a coal-fired power plant to 2.3 pounds for the new technology, a decrease of more than 85 percent. The new technology also should appreciably reduce the costs of smelting aluminum.

Yet another interesting case is the Chuquicamata copper smelter in northern Chile. As Figure 6-4 illustrates, during the 1980–1999 period this smelter increased the amount of recovered arsenic emissions from 35 to 90 percent and the amount of recovered sulfur dioxide emissions from zero to 80 percent. Codelco, the state enterprise that owns Chuquicamata, spent more than $600 million to realize these improvements. Though this is a formidable sum, Chuquicamata nevertheless managed to remain one of the world's largest and lowest-cost copper producers during this period.

Although the reduction in sulfur dioxide emissions at Chuquicamata is impressive, the technology exists today to capture more than 99 percent of these emissions. As a result, smelters in countries with very stringent environmental standards—Japan, for example—remove all but 1 or 2 percent of their sulfur dioxide emissions. Unfortunately, at the other end of the spectrum, a significant number of smelters still allow 100 percent of their emissions to escape into the atmosphere.

Thus, the impact of new technology on sulfur dioxide pollution is substantial where public policy internalizes these environmental costs and far less impressive elsewhere. Today, the best smelters are producing 100 tons of copper with less sulfur dioxide pollution than smelters generated in producing

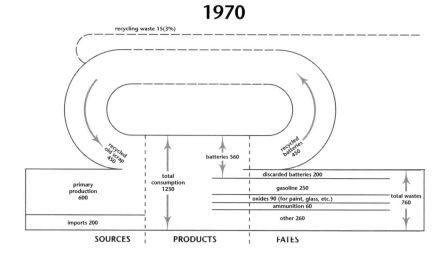

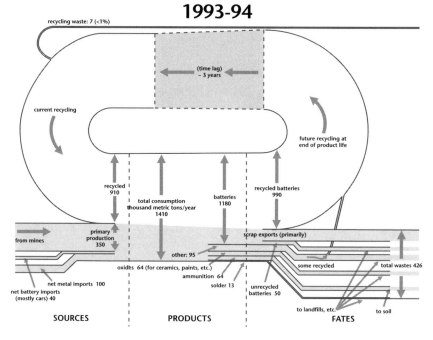

Figure 6-2. Lead Flows in the United States, 1970 and 1993–1994 (thousands of tons)

Source: Interagency Working Group on Industrial Ecology, Material, and Energy Flows, as reproduced in Brown and others 2000, 14.

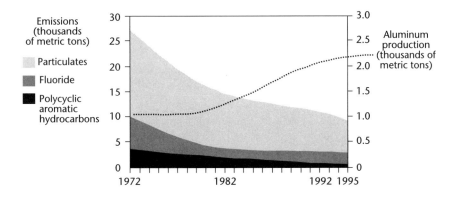

Figure 6-3. Production and Air Emissions for the Canadian Aluminum Industry, 1973–1995

Source: Ministère de l'Environnement et de la Faune du Québec, as cited in Aluminum Industry Association 1997.

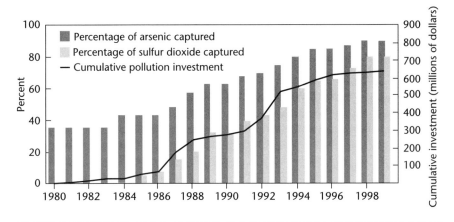

Figure 6-4. Percentage of Arsenic and Sulfur Dioxide Emissions Captured and Cumulative Investment in Pollution Abatement at the Chuquicamata Smelter, Chile, 1980–1999

Note: Figures for the years after 1995 are projections.

Source: Corporacion Nacional del Cobre de Chile (Codelco).

just one ton several decades ago. In addition, about a fourth of the world's copper is now produced by a new hydrometallurgical process, solvent extraction electrowinning, which completely bypasses the smelting stage of the traditional process. As a result, the copper it creates generates no sulfur dioxide emissions.

There are instances where environmental or other concerns may preclude mineral exploitation, where mining or mineral processing is simply incompatible with preserving environmental resources and other assets that society values highly. Activities that diminish the natural beauty of national parks, the pristine wilderness of remote areas, the culture and mores of indigenous people, and biodiversity are often cited examples.[5] In these situations, no amount of technological change may reduce the costs to acceptable levels, and public policy may quite appropriately place certain sites off limits to mineral exploitation.[6] This, in fact, has been the case for some time in most countries. Though making it more difficult for the cost-reducing effects of new technology to offset the cost-increasing effects of depletion, such exclusions, even when growing in magnitude, are not incompatible with falling resource costs, as recent history shows. We will return to this issue in Chapter 7.

Internalizing the Externalities

According to the preceding section, the technology currently exists to capture all or almost all of the sulfur dioxide emissions arising from copper smelting. Yet this technology has diffused quite unevenly around the world, largely reflecting the success or failure of public policy in internalizing environmental costs. This brings us back to the first of the conditions necessary to avoid an environmental constraint on the long-run availability of mineral commodities: namely, that public policy must force firms to pay most or all of the environmental and any other external costs associated with their activities. This, in turn, requires (1) that governments are able to identify and measure these costs with some degree of accuracy, and (2) that they possess the means and the will to force firms to pay them, or at least most of them.

Valuing Environmental and Other Social Goods

Market prices provide a good starting point for assessing the value of the labor, capital, and the other inputs used in the extraction and processing of mineral commodities. However, many social goods, including clean water, wilderness, indigenous cultures, and biodiversity, are not traded on markets, and therefore alternative means are needed to assess their value. During the past several decades, economists and others have devoted considerable effort to devising the necessary techniques.

One approach, a fairly recent social experiment noted above, entails the actual creation of markets for environmental goods. For example, the government has for some years now allowed U.S. coal-powered electric power utilities to trade sulfur dioxide permits. Those companies that can reduce their sulfur dioxide emissions at a cost less than the going permit price have an incentive to sell their permits. If the opposite is true, companies have an incentive to buy permits. So the market price for permits reflects the lowest possible cost to society of reducing sulfur dioxide emissions by one additional ton. If (and only if) the total number of permits reflects the optimum level of sulfur dioxide pollution, their price provides a good measure of the social costs associated with an additional ton of sulfur dioxide emissions. Perhaps of more importance, these permits force firms to internalize the costs of their sulfur dioxide emissions.

Other approaches depend on inferences from actual consumer behavior. For example, the difference in value between similar houses close to and away from an airport provides an estimate of the social cost, measured by what people are willing to pay in additional housing costs, of the noise pollution created by arriving and departing airplanes. Studies that measure the travel and other expenses people incur to use lakes, streams, and other recreational facilities similarly provide some indication of the value people place on such natural resources.

A third approach, contingent valuation, arose primarily to value a class of environmental goods prized for their nonuse or existence value. Many people, for example, may place a positive value on the rainforests of the Amazon, the pristine wilderness of Alaska, or the indigenous culture of the Bla'an people who live on the island of Mindanao in the Philippines.[7] This may be true even though they themselves never plan to visit the Amazon, Alaska, or the Philippines. Such nonuse value has in practice proven particularly difficult to measure. Contingent valuation attempts to do so by asking people, typically in a structured manner following certain guidelines, how much they would pay to preserve these resources. It has been used in the United States, both in policy evaluation and in legal cases for resource damage assessments, and elsewhere as well. It is generally considered the only available method for valuing environmental and other social assets with significant nonuse value.

Contingent valuation is, however, controversial, in part because it is not based on or even related to actual behavior. Those polled do not actually have to pay what they say they would pay. Among the experts, there is widespread agreement that poorly designed contingent valuation studies—for example, ones in which the respondents are inadequately informed or the questions are leading—can produce highly flawed results. There is much less agreement, however, about the reliability of well-designed studies (see Box 6-2).[8]

Critics fault contingent valuation at two very different levels. First, many claim that the methodology (asking people what they would pay) simply does not produce reliable responses for a host of reasons. Here, the complaint is that contingent valuation does not produce the information it purports to— namely, true willingness to pay.

Box 6-2. The Coronation Hill Project

Public acceptance, or rather the lack of it, can also be a serious problem for the use of contingent valuation. Cox (1994) provides an interesting example in his analysis of the public dispute in Australia over the proposed gold, platinum, and palladium mine at Coronation Hill. Largely because this deposit lies within the Kakadu Conservation Zone in the Northern Territory, the Australian government carried out an extensive cost–benefit analysis of the proposal. The study used contingent valuation to estimate the value of preserving the area. The analysis was conducted with considerable care, with the assistance of experts from abroad, and in accordance with accepted procedures. It found that the Australian people feel strongly about the possible environmental damage from mining in the Conservation Zone, but the study created such a fierce backlash from industry and other groups that the government removed all references to the contingent valuation effort from its final report.

Second, several critics (Humphreys 1992, 2000; Sagoff 2000; Soderholm and Sundqvist 2000) question the use of contingent valuation for more fundamental philosophical or ethical reasons. For them, even if contingent valuation does elicit reliable responses, adding the willingness to pay across all individuals in society is not the appropriate way for society to place a value on social goods.

They argue for an alternative approach, which recognizes that biodiversity, native cultures, pristine wilderness, and other social goods with substantial nonuse value are public goods, just like national defense or safe municipal drinking water. Though the latter could be valued using contingent valuation, this is not how governments make the budgetary decisions determining how much is spent on such public goods. Rather, these decisions are made through a political process that reconciles the various competing interests of society, not an artificially constructed simulation of the marketplace. These two processes are very different, and they may lead to very different results as well.

The political process allows a public debate. This provides individuals and organizations with the opportunity to make their own views known, as well as to become better informed about the issues and the views of others. The critics of contingent valuation also claim that the political process more readily accommodates the fact that individuals may make decisions about the purchase of private goods in a different way using different criteria than the decisions about public goods. As citizens, for example, individuals may support policies (such as higher taxes for education) that have no impact or even a negative impact on their own well-being. The political process, it is argued, is much more likely to take into account and reflect such support than contingent valuation.

To be sure, both approaches give the wealthy a greater say in the provision of public goods (because the rich have more dollars to spend on questions posed in contingent valuation studies and more dollars to spend influencing the political process). With the political process, however, every individual no matter how poor ultimately has one vote in electing public officials. This may leave the poor feeling less disenfranchised.

This review of various techniques for valuing environmental resources is far from comprehensive or complete, yet it suffices to show that measuring the full social costs associated with mineral exploitation is complex and difficult. Although our tools in this area have advanced considerably during the past several decades, much progress is still needed before reliable measures of environmental resource values are available, particularly for those resources with nonuse value.

The current debate over global warming and climate change, unfortunately, provides an excellent illustration of the need for progress in this area. After years of discussion, there is now a growing consensus that global warming is a reality, and that carbon dioxide and other greenhouse gases are largely responsible. Still hotly disputed, however, are the pace of climate change, the consequences and costs, the contribution of people as opposed to nature, and the benefits of curtailing industries and other human activities that generate greenhouse gases. These uncertainties make it difficult, if not impossible, to assess the external costs associated with the global warming that coal producers and other mineral firms generate. Yet some knowledge of these costs is needed before governments can implement an appropriate carbon tax or pursue other measures designed to internalize these externalities.

The Means and the Will

Once the environmental costs are determined—by valuation or political process—governments need the means and the will to force producers to pay these costs. For some countries—those in the early stages of development and those in transition from centrally planned to market economies—the required institutional capacity is still in need of development. For most countries, however, this is not a problem, and the means clearly exist. Indeed, as was noted above, the ongoing debate is over which set of tools or means governments should rely upon. Command-and-control regulations, probably the most common instrument, can require the use of certain technologies or equipment, and set ceilings on the permissible amounts of given pollutants. However, economic incentives, such as pollution taxes, have in recent years found increasing favor because they often lower the costs of reducing pollution. With both command-and-control regulations and economic incentives, there are enforcement problems, but these do not appear any greater than in many other areas of public policy, such as worker health and safety or taxation compliance.

The great differences noted above in the recovery of sulfur dioxide emissions found among copper smelters suggest that the will of governments to internalize costs may be a more serious problem. Of course, some of these differences may reflect the inadequate institutional capacity that impedes efforts in certain countries to internalize environmental and other social costs. Some of these differences may also reflect the lower environmental costs associated with copper smelting in more remote and less inhabited regions. Moreover, as old smelters are replaced over time, state-of-the-art environmental control technologies are likely to be used more widely. Thus some of the current discrepancies among smelters may be temporary. Yet, given the long lives of many copper smelters, "temporary" may mean many decades.

Still, the will of governments does appear problematic. The sorry environmental legacies of state-owned mining enterprises in Russia and other states with economies in transition raise some troubling concerns. Clearly, if the government has a conflict of interest—if it owns and operates mineral enterprises and is also responsible for ensuring that they adhere to acceptable environmental practices—the environment often suffers from a lack of will on the part of the government to internalize environmental and other social costs.

Another serious and possibly more permanent problem, given the recent trends away from central planning and toward the privatization of state-owned enterprises, entails artisanal or informal mining (see Box 6-3). Artisanal mines are highly inefficient, often leaving in the ground ore that better-run operations would exploit. They are more dangerous, and often employ women and children. They are also far more damaging to the environment per unit of output. Many gold operations, for example, discharge mercury into the surface water and groundwater, creating environmental hazards that affect their own workers as well as other people. Acid mine drainage, soil erosion, deforestation, and river silting are also common problems. Sites are typically abandoned with little or no reclamation.

In many respects, artisanal mining is resource exploitation at its worst, but it does provide a subsistence existence to millions of individuals with few if any alternatives. Governments, as a result, are reluctant to close down these operations—or even in many cases to impose environmental and other regulations. In short, artisanal mining represents a major social and political problem whose resolution largely awaits major new initiatives to eliminate poverty and the dearth of economic opportunities, which are ultimately responsible for these marginal activities so damaging to the environment.

Climate change provides another illustration of the problems society can encounter in its struggle to deal effectively with externalities. Even without

---

Box 6-3. Artisanal Mining

Artisanal mining is carried out on a very small scale—often illegally—by individuals or groups using the simplest and most primitive equipment. According to the International Labor Organization (1999), about 13 million people along with 100 million dependents worldwide depend on small-scale mining for their livelihood. Although some of these workers are engaged in small-scale mechanized mining, many are employed in the artisanal sector. The number of workers in small-scale mining rivals that of the formal mining sector, and has been growing at 20 percent a year during the past five years, a rate far faster than that for the formal mining sector.

Barry (1996, 3) estimates that artisanal mining accounts for 20 percent of the gold, 40 percent of the diamonds, and nearly all the gemstones produced in Africa. Somewhat less than half of Brazil's gold production comes from such operations, down from 70 percent just a few years ago. In addition to gold, diamonds, and gemstones, artisanal miners produce copper, silver, tin, zinc, and coal.

---

the uncertainties noted above, creating the political will on an international basis to curb greenhouse gases in a world of many independent nation-states is daunting. Developing countries claim that they did not create the problem and should not now have to slow their growth to reduce greenhouse emissions. The industrial world argues that selective cutbacks by only a few countries will not be effective. Still other countries may benefit from a warmer climate, or believe they may benefit, and so are not greatly inclined to support efforts to abate or reverse climate change. And all countries are reluctant to bear more of the costs than they believe is their fair share, which invariably is less than other countries propose. The possibilities for stalemate are obvious.

Conclusions

The shift in the ongoing debate over the long-run availability of nonrenewable mineral resources during the 1990s raises some interesting issues by focusing on the potential constraint that the environment and other external costs may impose on resource exploitation. In the past, scientists and engineers appear to have successfully generated the new technology and other innovations needed to offset the cost-increasing effects of depletion, as earlier chapters have shown.

In the future, if environmental and other social costs become a more important component of the total cost of mineral resource production and use, as seems likely, the favorable trend toward greater mineral resource availability can continue, as we have seen, but only if two conditions are satisfied. First, mineral producers with the assistance of science and technology must be able to continue to offset the upward pressure on their costs due to depletion. Second, public policy must internalize more of the environmental and other social costs of mineral production so that producers have incentives to reduce these costs as well as their other costs. Failure to force firms to pay for all or almost all of the social costs they generate undermines their motivation to develop and adopt new technologies that reduce these costs, and deprives society of the most effective weapon it possesses to mitigate the damage inflicted on the environment.

Of these two conditions, the second appears the most challenging. The pursuit of this condition will involve policy analysts, economists, political scientists, and other social scientists in the struggle to ensure the long-run availability of mineral commodities. Indeed, their role could turn out to be even more difficult than that of their colleagues in engineering and the natural sciences, for the problems of valuing environmental resources and the problems of ensuring that governments have the will and the capacity to internalize all the social costs may prove more troubling, perhaps far more troubling, than the more traditional technical challenges.

Notes

1. The extent to which such a situation has actually prevailed in the past, biasing the cost and price trends discussed in chapter 4, is unclear. Population growth, the rise in per capita income, and the growing exploitation of natural resources have in many parts of the world increased the demand to protect the environment. This shift in preferences has increased the external costs associated with the production and use of mineral commodities. The impact of this development, however, has been partially or totally offset by the growing use of environmental regulations and other public policies that force mineral commodity producers to internalize many erstwhile external costs.

2. The legislation specifically states that the allowances given to producers are not property rights in order to allow the government to reduce the number of allowances in the future without incurring suits from private firms claiming an unconstitutional "taking" of their property. In other respects, however, for all practical purposes the government allowances are property rights.

3. Where pollutants have a local or regional impact—as is the case with sulfur dioxide emissions—public policy, in addition to setting an overall ceiling, should ensure that emissions are not unduly concentrated in one or several locations after trading occurs.

4. PAHs, which arise from the incomplete combustion of carbon compounds, are largely the result of forest fires and the burning of wood. In the aluminum industry, the baking of pitch found in the anodes causes PAH emissions. In newer smelters using Soderberg anodes, PAH emissions are almost zero.

5. These are all situations in which the MEC curve in Figure 6-1 may lie above the MNB curve across all possible outputs.

6. It does not necessarily follow that exploration also should be excluded from all such sites. Exploration typically entails far less environmental damage than mine development and operation. It also provides information that permits a more accurate assessment of the potential benefits (the MNB curve) from mining in a particular area. Although this point may trouble those concerned about preserving wilderness areas, they may take comfort in the fact that few if any private firms are likely to have an interest in conducting exploration where the likelihood of being permitted to develop a successful discovery is questionable.

7. For an interesting description of the efforts by a mining company to preserve the Bla'an culture, see Davis 1998.

8. For a recent review of the debate over contingent valuation that contends most of the alleged shortcomings can be resolved, see Carson and others 2001.

References

Aluminum Industry Association. 1997. *The Canadian Aluminum Industry and the Environment.* Montreal: Aluminum Industry Association.

Barry, M. 1996. *Regularizing Informal Mining: A Summary of the Proceedings of the International Roundtable on Artisanal Mining.* Occasional Paper No. 6. Washington, DC: The World Bank, Industry and Energy Department.

Brown, W.M., and others. 2000. *Materials and Energy Flows in the Earth Science Century: A Summary of a Workshop Held by the USGS in November 1998.* U.S. Geological Survey Circular 1194. Denver, CO: U.S. Geological Information Services.

Carson, R.T., and others. 2001. Contingent Valuation: Controversies and Evidence. *Environmental and Resource Economics* 19: 173–210.

Cox, A. 1994. Land Access to Mineral Development in Australia. In *Mining and the Environment*, edited by R.G. Eggert. Washington, DC: Resources for the Future.

Davis, S.L. 1998. Engaging the Community at the Tampakan Copper Project: A Community Case Study in Resource Development with Indigenous People. *Natural Resources Forum* 22: 233–243.

Ellerman, A.D. 1999. The Next Restructuring: Environmental Regulation. *The Energy Journal* 20(1): 141–147.

Humphreys, D. 1992. *The Phantom of Full Cost Pricing*, A paper given at the International Council on Metals and the Environment seminar on full cost pricing. London: The RTZ Corporation PLC.

———. 2000. Taxing or Talking: Addressing Environmental Externalities in the Extractive Industries. *Minerals & Energy* 15(4): 33–40.

International Labor Organization (1999). *Social and Labour Issues in Small-Scale Mining.* Geneva: International Labour Office.

Mendonça, A. 1998. *The Use of the Contingent Valuation Method to Assess Environmental Cost of Mining in Serra dos Carajas: Brazilian Amazon Region*, Unpublished PhD dissertation. Golden, CO: Division of Economics and Business, Colorado School of Mines.

Mendonça, A., and J.E. Tilton. 2000. A Contingent Valuation Study of the Environmental Costs of Mining in the Brazilian Amazon. *Minerals & Energy* 15(4): 21–32.

Sagoff, M. 2000. Environmental Economics and the Conflation of Value and Benefit. *Environmental Science & Technology* 34(8): 1426–1432.

Soderholm, P., and T. Sundqvist. 2000. Ethical Limitations of Social Cost Pricing: An Application to Power Generation Externalities. *Journal of Economic Issues* 34(2): 453–462.

Stavins, R.N. 1998. What Can We Learn from the Grand Policy Experiment? Lessons from SO$_2$ Allowance Trading. *Journal of Economic Perspectives* 12(3): 69–88.

Van Leeuwen, T.M. 2000. *An Aluminum Revolution III*, Desk Notes, September 29. New York: Credit Suisse First Boston Corporation.

Chapter 7

Findings and Implications

During the past several decades, we have learned a great deal about the long-run availability of mineral commodities, thanks in large part to the lively debate among scholars and others over this important issue. We now know, for example, that the world is not likely to wake up one day to find the cupboard bare or the well dry. We will not run out of mineral commodities the way a car runs out of gasoline: one minute speeding along the highway, the next completely stranded on the berm. Depletion, if it becomes a serious problem, will raise the real costs of finding and producing mineral commodities, but probably slowly yet persistently over years and decades. There likely will be signs of impending scarcity long before there actually are serious shortages.

This is because the mineral resources that provide for society's material and energy needs vary greatly in quality. The high-quality, low-cost resources currently being exploited account for only a fraction of the total. Once they are gone, large amounts of lower quality resources will remain, which in the absence of offsetting technological change would be more expensive to find and exploit. Long before the lowest-quality resources—the last ounce of silver or the last ton of coal in the earth's crust—are used, costs would become prohibitive.

So depletion raises the specter of a world where resources are too costly to use rather than a world with no resources. This means that the opportunity-cost paradigm rather than the fixed-stock paradigm is the appropriate way to assess the long-run availability of mineral commodities. This finding leads to two important corollaries.

First, depletion is no longer inevitable. Although, over time, depletion tends to drive up the costs and prices of mineral commodities, new technology tends to mitigate this tendency. Indeed, mineral commodities can become more available over time if the cost-reducing effects of new technology more than offset the cost-increasing effects of depletion.

Second, measures of availability should reflect the sacrifice that society makes to obtain additional quantities of mineral commodities. Possible indicators of the sacrifice include user costs, production costs, and prices. Prices are the most common measure encountered because they are readily available, and because they reflect trends in both user costs and production costs. Although these three measures suffer from various shortcomings, and may even at times move in opposite directions, they provide far more useful insights regarding availability trends than fixed-stock measures, such as the life expectancies of reserves or the resource base.

We also now know that new technology has during the past 130 years kept the adverse effects of depletion at bay despite an unprecedented surge in both population and the consumption of mineral commodities. Real production costs and prices for many mineral commodities have actually fallen, implying that their availability has increased.

Of course, there have also been shortages. Indeed, shortages have occurred with some regularity for a number of reasons—wars, strikes, economic booms, cartels, insufficient investment in new mines and processing facilities, and perverse government policies—but depletion is not among them. This is fortunate, and it is why the shortages the world has so far experienced have not endured for long.

Two clouds or caveats, however, cast a shadow over this fairly rosy picture. First, we know that the past is not necessarily a good guide to the future. Although the current levels and rates of accumulation of mineral reserves augurs well for the next several decades, the more distant future is much harder to discern. We simply do not have the tools to forecast the future course of technological change with any semblance of the accuracy needed to know whether it will suffice to offset the adverse effects of depletion.[1]

Second, our measures of availability take into account only the costs that producers incur and the prices that their customers recognize and pay. Environmental and other external costs associated with the production and use of mineral commodities are not considered. At any point in time, this omission imparts a downward bias in our availability measures, causing them to understate the true costs and prices of mineral commodities.

How it affects trends over time, however, is less clear. It must be admitted that the tendency for environmental costs to grow in importance and as a percentage of total costs causes our availability measures more and more to overestimate availability and to underestimate scarcity. Conversely, the considerable efforts that governments around the world have made during the past several decades to force companies and consumers to pay for more of what were formerly external costs has partially, and perhaps totally, offset this upward bias.

As for the future, some believe that rising environmental and other social costs may preclude the widespread production and use of mineral commodities, forcing governments to impose regulations and other policies that greatly restrict their use. We have seen that this need not be the case, but only if public policy more completely internalizes the external costs, and if society can continue, as it has in the past, to generate the technology needed to keep mineral commodity costs (which would now include all the social costs) from rising.

Unfortunately, satisfying both of these two necessary conditions is neither easy nor certain. True, recent history suggests that environmental and other social costs, once firms are required to pay them, may be just as amenable to the cost-reducing effects of new technology as other costs. However, internalizing these costs may not be easy for two reasons. First, considerable progress is still needed to develop acceptable techniques for measuring the value of the environment, indigenous cultures, and other social goods. This is particularly so for those goods with substantial non-use value, and where different groups within society hold conflicting value systems that lead to greatly different preferences. Second, the political will to force firms to pay for all the social assets they use may falter, especially in regions where unemployment and poverty are already widespread, but elsewhere as well.

So, despite all that we have learned about the long-run availability of mineral commodities, the central question remains unanswered. We simply do not know whether or not coming generations face a future of mineral commodity shortages. Those who argue otherwise ask the rest of us to share their faith, or lack of faith, in technology. This is why the debate continues.

More geologic information on the incidence and nature of mineral deposits, particularly subeconomic mineral deposits, could go a long way toward resolving this critical issue by providing useful insights on the nature and shape of cumulative supply curves. The needed knowledge, however, is not currently available, nor is it likely to soon become available, largely because little economic incentive exists to learn more about deposits whose profitable exploitation at best lies many years in the future.

Despite this somewhat frustrating state of affairs, important implications still flow from what we do know about the long-run availability of mineral commodities—implications for sustainable development; for green accounting; for indigenous cultures and other social goods; for conservation, recycling, and renewable resource use; and for population, poverty, and discrimination.

Sustainable Development

Sustainable development is a term with many meanings. The World Commission on Environment and Development, better known as the Brundtland Commission after its chair, Gro Harlem Brundtland, is widely credited with introducing the term *sustainable development* into the public lexicon in its report *Our Common Future*. This volume defines sustainable development as development that "meets the needs of the present without compromising the ability of future generations to meet their own needs" (World Commission on Environment and Development 1987, 8).

Since then, as Toman (1992) and other writers have noted, many other definitions have surfaced. For some, sustainable development means protecting a particular ecosystem, for others preserving biodiversity, and for still others protecting an indigenous culture or a local community from the development of a nearby mine. Then there are those who see sustainable development as helping a mining community remain economically viable after the ore is gone and the mines are closed. In yet another use, sustainable development is the equitable distribution of income, goods, and resources among different countries and people today, and so is void of any intertemporal dimension.

Here we use sustainable development to mean that the present generation behaves in a way that does not preclude future generations from enjoying a standard of living at least comparable to that of its own. This definition is fairly common among economists. Like the original definition of the Brundtland Commission, it has a macro orientation, focusing on changes in the welfare of society as a whole over time rather than the well-being of a particular ecosystem or local community.

Our concern, specifically, is the possibility that the current consumption of mineral commodities may force future generations to accept a lower standard of living. Though sustainable development has emerged as a popular concern only during the past decade or two, fears of resource exhaustion as we have seen date back at least to the eighteenth-century writings of Thomas Malthus and the Classical economists. We care about the long-run availability of mineral commodities for many reasons, but the primary reason is presumably the widespread belief that growing scarcity could threaten the welfare of future generations.

Upon some reflection, however, the link between the long-run availability of mineral commodities and sustainable development turns out to be much looser than one might at first suspect. This is because the potential for future generations to enjoy a standard of living equal to that of the present generation depends on all the assets that we pass on. Abundant low-cost mineral resources are just one of these assets. Others include human-made or physical capital (houses, factories, schools, office buildings, roads, bridges, and other infrastructure), human capital (a healthy, well-educated populace), natural capital (a clean environment, pristine wilderness, and rich biodiversity), political and social institutions (stable and democratic government, a well-developed legal system, and a tradition of resolving conflict by peaceful means), culture (literature, music, art, and dance), and of course technology.

As a result, increasing the availability of mineral commodities may make sustainable development somewhat easier to achieve, but certainly does not ensure it. A generation that fails to invest in new technology, that despoils the environment, and that perpetuates widespread poverty in order to husband its stock of mineral resources for future use is not likely to achieve sustainable development, and is even less likely to earn accolades from future generations.

Yet sustainable development is possible even with declining long-run availability of mineral commodities. It simply requires an offsetting increase in the other assets passed on to future generations. Indeed, future generations may even benefit from an increase in the current exploitation of mineral commodities if it allows today's generation to spend more on infrastructure, education, research and development, and other types of investments (see Box 7-1).

In either case, the pace of mineral extraction appears at best to be but a modest determinant of sustainable development. Much more important is how much the current generation squanders on wars, corruption, needless mismanagement, and other welfare-reducing activities. Also of great importance is how much of its welfare-increasing expenditures the current generation devotes to its own consumption and how much it invests.

During the past century, the production of mineral commodities has exploded, yet their long-run availability has increased, thanks largely to the investment in research and development that has generated a continuing flow of new technologies. This investment, coupled with society's other investments, has left each succeeding generation better off than that of its parents—at least in industrial countries.

This raises two intriguing issues. First, though sustainable development has become the holy grail by which much public policy and behavior currently are judged, is it perhaps too modest a goal? Do we not want the generation of our children and grandchildren to be substantially better off than we are, just as our generation is substantially better than those of our parents and grandparents? Have we perhaps set our sights too low?

Second, how much should the present generation be saving and how much should it be investing? Although it is easy to point to instances of profligate consumption by others, particularly by those richer than we, poverty is also widespread. A large portion of the world's current population does not have adequate food, housing, medical care, or education. In deciding how much of our current income to invest for future generations, how do we weigh and compare intergenerational and intragenerational equity? The issue

---

Box 7-1. Strong versus Weak Substitutability

Going one (big) step further, some economists (Solow 1974; Hartwick 1977; Dasgupta and Heal 1979) have even argued that sustainable development is possible with the complete exhaustion of nonrenewable mineral commodities, using models with strong substitutability assumptions. These assumptions allow the substitution of other inputs for nonrenewable mineral resources in the production of all critical goods. Conversely, it is not surprising that models with weak substitutability assumptions—which allow for some substitution but not the complete elimination of mineral commodities in the production of goods and services—find the complete exhaustion of mineral resources incompatible with sustainable development. Advocates of the latter set of models (Daly 1996; Ruth 1995; Neumayer 2000) argue with some persuasion that the strong substitutability assumption defies the laws of nature.

However, the debate over strong and weak substitutability, though of some intellectual interest, may be of questionable practical relevance. As was pointed out in the text above, physical exhaustion is not the issue. We will not literally run out of resources. Scarcity may push the costs of some mineral commodities sufficiently high to preclude their widespread use, but resources will remain in the ground, and so will be available at some price. Higher prices, as we have seen, increase the challenge of achieving sustainable development, but do not necessarily preclude it.

---

is further complicated by the fact that providing food, housing, medical care, and education to today's poor is also an investment in the future. We return to this important issue when examining the implications of resource availability for population.

Green Accounting

Among the great economic inventions of the twentieth century are modern national income and product accounts. Income accounts, such as the well-known gross domestic product (GDP), measure the total income and output of a nation during a year or some other period. Asset accounts indicate the assets, liabilities, and net worth of a nation at a particular point in time.

National income and product accounts provide a useful report card on a country's economic performance. Is output growing? Is the ratio of investment to consumption rising or falling? How does this ratio compare with that of other countries? Are the country's total assets growing? Are some regions expanding faster than others? How is total income divided among labor, capital, and other resource owners? Such information is of intrinsic interest, and it is invaluable for the formation of public policy.

National income and product accounts do, however, suffer from a number of deficiencies. With a few exceptions, for example, they have traditionally considered as income and output only sales and purchases that occur in the marketplace. They thus take account of the services provided by a paid maid or housekeeper, but not the services of an unpaid housespouse. Thus many welfare-creating activities are excluded.

Another important shortcoming concerns their treatment of natural resources and the environment. They currently take into account the production of mineral commodities and their flows through the economy, but completely ignore changes in the stocks of mineral assets in the ground. So while the accumulation and depreciation of physical assets (e.g., plant and equipment) are counted, the discovery of new mineral reserves and their depletion over time are overlooked. This anomaly is troubling, because mineral resources are often important inputs into the production of goods and services, just like labor and capital. The treatment of environmental assets is even more of a problem. Not only are changes in these important assets ignored in the asset accounts; they are largely overlooked in the income and product accounts as well.

These shortcomings mean that a country could conceivably be enjoying strong apparent economic growth—on the basis of the exploitation of its natural resources and environmental assets—that was unsustainable and actually impoverishing the country. A full reckoning of the costs and benefits would reflect a country not growing stronger economically, but rather living off its natural resource and environmental assets.

Green accounting encompasses the efforts during the past several decades in the United States and abroad to augment the traditional treatment of the environment and natural resources in national income and product accounts. It is related to sustainable development, in the sense that a well-designed green accounting system should indicate whether or not a particular economy is developing in a sustainable manner.

In the case of mineral resources, green accounting efforts have produced various procedures for estimating the value of reserves in the ground. These techniques, described in some detail in Nordhaus and Kokkelenberg (1999, ch. 3), attempt in various ways to estimate the value of the user costs (or Hotelling rent) plus the Ricardian rent associated with existing reserves, as illustrated in Figure 3-2.

These efforts indicate that U.S. mineral wealth has changed little during the past several decades. This means that the value of reserve additions, plus any revaluation of reserves due to price changes, have more or less offset the value of reserve depletions over time. This provides little support for the view that the country is in the midst of an unsustainable mineral resource consumption binge, though several decades is perhaps too short a period of time for assessing this proposition.

Another interesting result flowing from this work concerns the relatively modest contribution of mineral resources to the total wealth of the United States. The value of U.S. mineral resources is estimated at only 3 to 7 percent of the country's tangible capital stock (Nordhaus and Kokkelenberg 1999, 104). Adding in other assets, such as human capital, would further reduce these figures.

Even of more interest is the somewhat perverse relationship between a country's mineral wealth and the long-run availability of mineral commodities. Although logic would suggest that an increase in mineral availability should increase mineral wealth, this is rarely the case. Again, referring back to Figure 3-2, we can see that an increase in a mineral commodity's price, a sign of growing mineral commodity scarcity, increases the Ricardian rent associated with existing reserves, and hence the value of mineral reserves in the ground.

Alternatively, consider the impact of a new technological development that made it possible to capture British thermal units (Btus) from solar energy more cheaply than from mining and burning coal. The costs of Btu production, which previously might be reflected by the step function in Figure 3-2, would now be replaced by a horizontal line located below the costs of the lowest-cost coal mine. Coal deposits would no longer have any value, and solar energy would enjoy neither Ricardian rent nor user costs (Hotelling rents) because the available supply would have a common cost of production and would be limitless for all practical purposes. Although greatly improving the long-run availability of energy, this dramatic development would completely wipe out the mineral wealth once enjoyed by the owners of coal deposits. Nor would this loss be offset by new mineral wealth, because the new source of energy—solar power—would create neither Ricardian rent nor user costs.[2] Nevertheless, this magical development would increase the productive capacity of the world, and thus create other forms of wealth. Society would be better off.

Perhaps a more realistic example concerns the discovery and development of high-grade, low-cost copper deposits in Chile during the past couple of decades. By keeping the world price of copper below what it otherwise would have been, these new mines have reduced the value of copper reserves in the United States and elsewhere. The increased value of the reserves in Chile may or may not have offset losses elsewhere. But the new mines in Chile, by reducing the world price, have clearly increased the long-run availability of copper worldwide.

Mineral Extraction and Incompatible Social Goods

Indigenous cultures, biodiversity, and pristine wilderness are all examples of social goods that many contend are simply incompatible with the extraction of mineral commodities. Where this is true, internalizing the costs of these social goods more than merely reduces the optimal output of mineral resources—it reduces it to zero. How then can society protect these social goods without at the same time inducing unacceptable long-run scarcity of mineral commodities?

As Chapter 6 noted, public policy has for years prohibited mineral production in certain areas, such as national parks and military reservations. Moreover, the total size of these areas has expanded greatly during the past several decades, while simultaneously the availability of many mineral commodities has increased. This suggests that the protection of social goods incompatible with mining is possible without necessarily causing scarcity, though clearly the more territory withdrawn from mineral extraction the greater the challenge for new technology in the struggle to keep mineral costs and prices from rising.

The issue for public policy is not between choosing biodiversity, pristine wilderness, and indigenous culture on the one hand or the availability of mineral commodities on the other. It is not an either–or issue, a case of black or white, but rather a question of the appropriate trade-off. How much biodiversity, wilderness, and indigenous culture does society want to preserve? As the amount increases, so does the price to society in terms of the long-run mineral availability sacrificed. At the same time, as the amount increases, the additional or marginal benefits to society will fall, assuming the most valuable sites for biodiversity, wilderness, and indigenous culture are selected for protection first.

This suggests that public policy should continue to preserve these social goods, and exclude mining from the areas required, up to the point where the marginal costs (in terms of the resource availability sacrificed) just equals the marginal benefits to society. Such a policy may or may not give rise to the scarcity of mineral commodities in the long run, but if it does, the policy still promotes the welfare of society as a whole.

Moreover, some economists and policy analysts urge a cautionary policy— one that requires governments, when weighing the benefits and costs, to take account of the fact that once mining or other activities destroy such social goods, the damage is often irreversible. Moreover, as population and per capita income increase over time, the demand for these goods is likely to grow more rapidly than the demand for most other goods. Unlike other commodities, it is difficult or impossible to produce goods widely considered as close substitutes for biodiversity, indigenous cultures, and pristine wilderness.

Such concerns, coupled with the vast quantities of resources that are close to being economic and that are known to exist for many mineral commodities, suggest that a prudent policy at least for the present would preclude mineral development wherever important social goods are threatened. For example, the troubled history of the Panguna mine on Bougainville Island in Papua

New Guinea in retrospect indicates that the central government and private companies should have paid more attention to the concerns of the local people (see Box 7-2). Some might even argue that the mine should never have been developed, because it is simply too disruptive to the indigenous culture. Despite the attractive nature of this deposit, had this been the case, the effect on the long-run evolution of costs in the world copper industry would have been negligible. Indeed, given the large number of known but undeveloped porphyry deposits that could produce copper at costs close to many of today's operating mines, a number of mines could have been excluded from development with little effect on the long-run costs of producing copper.

Conservation, Recycling, and Renewable Resources

Concern over the long-run availability of mineral commodities has fostered, and continues to foster, widespread support for public policies and other activities that encourage conservation, recycling and secondary production, and where possible the greater use of renewable resources. Even if the long-run availability of mineral commodities is unknown, such policies, it is argued, are desirable as useful insurance in the event future shortages do arise.

Some even contend that these activities are inevitable. The world, they argue, is in the midst of what has to be a temporary period, as it exploits at an unprecedented rate its stocks of nonrenewable mineral resources. Once this era of profligate use draws to an end, as it must, there will be no choice. The world will have to rely far more on conservation, recycling, and renewable resources, and rising mineral commodity prices will provide the incentives to do so.

Although these positions are often advanced as self-evident and uncontroversial, they do raise a number of issues. The remainder of this section looks

---

Box 7-2. The Panguna Mine

The Panguna Mine began operations in 1972. CRA, a large Australian mining company that is now part of Rio Tinto Limited, developed and operated the mine, which in addition to copper produced significant quantities of gold. Although the company worked closely with the central government in Port Morseby, the local people on Bougainville Island became more and more hostile over time. They believed that they shared inadequately in the benefits while suffering most of the environmental and other costs associated with the mine's operations. They resorted to violence and forced the mine to close abruptly in 1989. Despite considerable remaining reserves, the mine has not reopened.

first at conservation, and then turns to recycling and the substitution of renewable resources.

Conservation

Conservation can be an elusive concept. To most people, it simply means using less. But this loose definition raises the question: How much less? At one extreme—which few conservationists would advocate, and which in any case would garner little public support—conservation could mean doing completely without.

At the other extreme, conservation could mean using mineral commodities efficiently without needless waste. If mineral commodities are properly priced, the marketplace should ensure they are used efficiently. In this case, no public policies or extra efforts to reduce mineral commodity use should be necessary. In practice, as Chapter 6 pointed out, prices for mineral commodities often do not include all the costs that their production and use impose on the environment and other social goods. In such cases, public policy is needed to ensure that these external costs are internalized. Here again, few are likely to object, at least in principle, to such efforts.

Conservation becomes more controversial when it entails reducing the use of mineral commodities below the levels that market efficiency dictates. Now, society is paying a price for conservation in less output and slower growth. As noted above, one might justify these costs as an insurance premium against the risk of future resource scarcity. This presumes, however, that there are no more cost-effective methods of buying insurance. This may not be the case. The prospects for adequate future supplies might be enhanced much more by devoting the income that would be lost as a result of conservation to developing new technologies to find and process mineral commodities.

Another possible reason for reducing current income to promote conservation rests on the belief that much of today's materialistic lifestyle in rich countries is not only unnecessary but undesirable, particularly because it may increase the likelihood of future mineral shortages. Thus, a decline in income that discourages undesirable consumption can be accommodated at little or no cost to society as a whole.

Despite some intuitive appeal, this argument raises at least four difficult issues. First, how do we decide what are necessary and desirable expenditures, once individual preferences as expressed through the marketplace are rejected as appropriate indicators? Do we make such decisions collectively through the political process? If so, if current consumption patterns are truly perverse, why has public policy not already introduced luxury taxes or other measures sufficient to correct the situation? Second, once this issue is resolved and we identify which expenditures are unnecessary and undesirable, might it not be preferable to divert the resources used to produce them to other contemporary needs, such as housing, food, and medical care for the poor?

Third, as we have seen, natural capital in the form of mineral resources is just one of many assets the current generation will pass on, affecting the welfare of future generations. If we are concerned about intergenerational equity and the welfare of future generations, public policy should encourage the current generation to consume less and invest more. Investments might be made in education and human capital, in the strengthening of social and cultural institutions, or in the body of scientific knowledge and technology. Only under special conditions is the best investment likely to entail primary emphasis on preserving mineral resources by conservation. Fourth, as was noted above, it is not clear that equity is served by augmenting the welfare of future generations at the expense of the current generation, given the widespread poverty that currently afflicts large parts of the globe and the tendency during the past century in industrial countries for each succeeding generation to be better off than its predecessor.

Pulling together these various thoughts, we can make a strong case for conservation, if conservation means using mineral commodities efficiently up to the point at which the costs (including all the social costs) of using another unit just equal the benefits to society. Moreover, so defined, the marketplace should encourage the efficient level of conservation as long as government policy forces producers and consumers to pay for all the costs. Over time, if scarcity drives up the prices of mineral commodities, conservation will cause their use to decline. Alternatively, if scarcity should decline, allowing prices to fall, conservation so defined will dictate an increase in the optimal use of mineral commodities. If conservation means something other than the efficient use of mineral commodities—as was the case, for example, with the conservation movement described in Chapter 2—it becomes more difficult to justify and more controversial.

Recycling and Secondary Production

Recycling and secondary production constitute an important source of supply for many metals, and they are often perfect substitutes for primary output. So by increasing recycling, society can slow the rate at which primary mineral resources are exploited. This does not mean, however, that all the metal in products coming to the end of their useful lives should be recycled. The lead once added to gasoline still exists, and in theory it could be recycled. In such dissipated uses, however, scrap metal is prohibitively expensive to recycle.

What then is the optimal amount of recycling that society should undertake, and to what extent is government intervention in the marketplace needed to achieve this optimum? One position, which parallels the efficiency criterion for conservation, contends that the output of copper, lead, tin, or any other metal should be divided between primary and secondary production so that total production costs are minimized. This means continuing to recycle up to the point at which the cost of obtaining one more ton of metal from recycling just equals the costs of producing one more ton from mining. Again, in both instances, all costs should be included, including environmental costs.

Some scholars who favor this view argue that public policy needs to encourage recycling, because primary production gets more subsidies in various forms and imposes more external costs on society than secondary production. This is not easy to actually demonstrate, particularly in light of the many efforts during the past decade or two to promote recycling. However, to the extent that public policy does discriminate in favor of primary production, a strong case can be made for eliminating this discrimination and thus for promoting more recycling.

Others contend that public policy should go further. Whether recycling is economic or not, they point out, often depends on the behavior of consumers. If consumers are conscientious and sort their waste (e.g., separating out metal cans), recycling becomes much more competitive. Educating consumers, as with education in general, is a type of public good. By reducing the costs of recycling, it provides benefits to society that at best recycling firms can capture only in part. If such external benefits exist, markets will fail, providing less of a good or service than is optimal from the point of view of society. This is the primary rationale for government support of education and of research and development. As a result, the argument goes, the government has a legitimate role to play in encouraging consumer behavior that promotes recycling.[3] Of course, public policy should take into account the value of the time and effort that households expend in their recycling efforts, as well as the satisfaction that many socially conscious individuals derive from such efforts.

Perhaps the most common and problematic case for policies favoring recycling contends that secondary production buys society time. According to this argument, as the world moves, as it must, from a cowboy economy based on nonrenewable resources to a spaceship economy based on renewable resources and secondary production, secondary production slows depletion. This extends the period available for the world to navigate through this difficult transition period, and reduces the resulting dislocation and hardship.[4]

We have seen, however, that depletion is not a question of the physical availability of mineral resources, but rather of costs. Should depletion eventually drive the costs of primary production up greatly, then the world will have to make the transition from nonrenewable primary resources to renewable resources and secondary production. However, forcing society to incur these costs now can be questioned for at least two reasons. First, although primary mineral commodities may become scarce in the long run, this is not certain. Why pay to alleviate a problem that may not arise? Why not pay when and if the problem actually occurs?[5]

Second, even if scarcity were certain, the income lost by pushing recycling beyond the point that minimizes the total production costs for mineral commodities might be better spent in other ways. Promoting technologies that reduce the costs of finding and producing mineral commodities or that develop suitable alternatives, for example, may be a far more effective strategy for mitigating the impact of depletion. More generally, investing these funds by attacking poverty, strengthening institutions, reducing corruption, and enhancing political stability may, as we have seen, pay far greater dividends to future generations, as compensation for our possible failure to maintain the long-run availability of mineral commodities.

The above, it is important to note, does not necessarily preclude public support for recycling. It does imply, however, that the case for such support is not self-evident, but rather requires empirical verification.

Renewable Resources

Solar power, biomass, and other renewable resources are replenishable on a time scale of relevance to humanity, and so can be used indefinitely. Does this mean, as is sometimes argued, that society should promote the use of renewable resources in place of nonrenewable ones?

The answer to this question closely parallels the preceding discussions of conservation and recycling. A strong case for market failure and government intervention favoring renewable over nonrenewable resources exists if the production and use of nonrenewables imposes greater external costs, or in other ways receives subsidies that exceed those bestowed on the production and use of renewables. Of course, if careful analyses of relative subsidies document that renewables are actually favored, then government policy should tilt in the opposite direction.

Government policies that favor the use of renewable resources beyond such measures are more difficult to justify, because they reduce income and wealth. This cost helps mitigate a problem that may in the end not arise. In addition, the income and wealth given up by the current generation might, if spent in other ways, enhance the welfare of future generations even more.

This seems particularly true because renewable resources can also suffer from depletion if use exceeds sustainable levels. A cursory glance at the resources generating the greatest concerns at the beginning of the twenty-first century finds the focus largely on renewables—climate, the ozone layer, water, air, soils, whales, and biodiversity in general. The general perception that renewables are sustainable but nonrenewables are not is clearly incorrect. Indeed, with renewables physical exhaustion is in some instances a real threat, as the extinction of many animal species during the past century illustrates. For this reason, the terms *renewable resources* and *nonrenewable resources* are misleading. Both can suffer from depletion, and in the case of renewables depletion may entail more than just rising costs.

Population, Poverty, and Discrimination

This final section explores the fascinating relationship between the long-run availability of mineral commodities and the world's population. In particular, it focuses on two issues. The first concerns the influence of resource availability on population, and addresses the question: To what extent does the availability of mineral commodities impose an upper limit or ceiling on the world's population? The second examines the influence of population on resource availability, and considers the question: Is a growing population a threat to the long-run availability of mineral commodities?

The Population Ceiling

At any particular time, available world resources do impose an upper limit on the number of people the world can support. Malthus and other Classical economists, as we saw in Chapter 2, recognized this fact more than 200 years ago. According to the law of diminishing returns, as more of a variable input (people) is added to a fixed input (land or resources in general), the additional return or output from adding one more unit of the variable input must at some point decline. Eventually, this decline will push the average output per person down until it just equals the subsistence level. At this point, which Malthus recognized was not a pleasant situation, the world reaches the upper limit on the number of people it can sustain.

Four aspects of this scenario, however, deserve further clarification. First, the optimal population level is significantly below the maximum possible. There are many reasons for this, including the fact that a world where everyone just barely manages to survive is not particularly enticing. There is far less consensus, however, on just what the optimum level of population is. Like beauty or equity, it is in the eye of the beholder, and so varies from individual to individual. For many, the optimum is less than the world's current population. For others, the ceiling is at or above this number.

Second, the world clearly possesses sufficient supplies of mineral commodities to support its current population of more than 6 billion, because it is doing so. Moreover, at some income level, it presumably will be able to support the 9 to 10 billion people expected by the middle of this century, when current forecasts see the world's population peaking. Less clear is how far developing countries can move toward the high living standards currently prevailing in industrial countries in light of these population figures and the long-run availability of mineral commodities. This, however, is a concern more relevant to the optimal level of population than to the ceiling. Moreover, although economic development is still poorly understood and appears to depend on the fortunate confluence of many factors, the long-run availability of mineral commodities does not appear to be of overwhelming importance. South Korea, Hong Kong, Singapore, Malaysia, Chile, and more recently China have all enjoyed rapid rates of economic growth during the past several decades, while many other developing countries have not—even though in a growing global economy all have more or less equal access to needed mineral commodities.

Third, renewable as well as nonrenewable resources impose a ceiling on population. Indeed, the availability of land, water, and other renewables may well constrain population growth long before nonrenewables, the latter's finite nature notwithstanding. If so, the mineral constraint on population is nonbinding, and hence largely or totally irrelevant.

Fourth, the population ceiling arising from mineral commodities is not stationary but rather shifts over time, responding to changes in their long-run availability. If new technology continues to offset the cost-increasing effects of depletion, the ceiling on population imposed by mineral resources could rise indefinitely. Growing scarcity would have the opposite effect.

So the answer to the first question is: Yes, the availability of mineral commodities does impose a limit on the world's population. Though true, and of some interest, this fact has limited significance in practice—in part because the ceiling is constantly changing, in part because renewable resources may dictate an even lower population limit, in part because the ceiling is above the current level of population and above those levels likely to prevail over the foreseeable future, and most important because the desired or optimal level of population is far below the ceiling and is set largely by other considerations.

The Population Threat

This brings us to the second question: Is population growth a significant threat to the long-run availability of mineral commodities? Here again the conventional wisdom, that the answer to this question is yes, is at best only partially correct. It is true that an increase in population, everything else remaining the same, tends to increase the demand for mineral commodities and so drives society up its cumulative supply curve at a faster pace than would otherwise be the case. However, as Julian Simon (1981, 1990) has so persistently argued, people influence the supply as well as the demand for mineral commodities. The more people, the more minds to develop the innovations and new technologies that shift the cumulative supply curve down over time. Whether the existence of more people on balance promotes or impedes the long-run availability of mineral commodities is an open question requiring empirical evidence for its resolution. Simon contends that a growing population increases availability, thanks to the ingenuity and resourcefulness of people; others are less sanguine.

Although controlled experiments of the kind so common in physics, chemistry, and other natural sciences are difficult to replicate in the social sciences, the past century does in a way provide a laboratory for an empirical test. Between 1900 and 2000, world population more than tripled, rising from less than 2 billion to more than 6 billion. Yet according to the measures reviewed above, resource availability did not significantly decline. This provides little support for the hypothesis that population growth seriously threatens the long-run availability of mineral commodities. Although the future could be a different story, those who advocate slowing population growth to preserve the long-run availability of mineral commodities need at least to ponder the possibility that they may unwittingly be pushing counterproductive policies.

The influence that people have on the supply of mineral commodities via their ingenuity and influence raises some other intriguing and even paradoxical issues. Poverty and discrimination, for instance, may be a far more serious challenge to the availability of mineral commodities than population per se. The World Bank (2001) estimates that poverty afflicts one in four people living in the developing world, or 1.2 billion individuals, where poverty means living on less than $1 a day. Without adequate housing, food, health care, and education, these individuals simply do not have the opportunity to develop the skills and talents needed to promote the technologies that push the cumulative supply curve down over time, or to contribute to society in other ways.

This reflects a loss that makes the entire world, industrial as well as developing, poorer than it otherwise would be. How many Leonardo DaVincis, Thomas Edisons, and Albert Einsteins have lived and died in the slums of Calcutta, Rio de Janeiro, and New York lacking the means to develop their extraordinary talents? How much better off would the world in general be without poverty, and how much more available would mineral commodities be in particular?

Discrimination poses an equally troubling problem. Around the world, women and minorities are denied opportunities to obtain the education and experience needed to pursue productive professional careers. Like poverty, discrimination affects us all, not just those afflicted. Like poverty, it does so in a particularly insidious way, by preventing what might have been. As a result, those who are not directly affected have little or no idea of the magnitude of the losses they suffer. Indeed, many are unaware that poverty and discrimination also impoverish them.

Although there is no way to assess accurately these costs, they must be huge. Between a third and a fourth of humanity currently is unable to contribute to the welfare of society as a result of poverty and discrimination. If these or higher figures apply to the past as well—not an unreasonable assumption—they suggest that the benefits the world enjoys from the stock of existing technology (to say nothing of the those flowing from the arts and humanities) might now be 20 to 40 percent greater. In the case of mineral commodities, such an additional infusion of new technology would have accentuated the tendency during the past century toward increasing availability, and enhanced the prospects for the continuation of this favorable trend in the future.

These issues suggest that the frequent accusations leveled by many against industrial countries, and in particular against the United States—that their profligate use of mineral commodities is inequitable and unjust—may be misguided. Although the per capita consumption of mineral commodities in China, India, Nigeria, and other developing countries is quite low, the widespread poverty in these countries means they can contribute only modestly to the ongoing struggle to offset the cost-increasing effects of depletion. Industrial countries, however, despite their apparently profligate use, are in a far stronger position to foster the long-run availability of mineral commodities. If the unrestrained use of mineral commodities also helps generate the income that supports the development of new cost-reducing technologies, it may actually benefit developing countries, despite the claims to the contrary.

Some may find this idea disturbing. They can, perhaps, take comfort in the fact that its underlying logic also leads to the conclusion that industrial countries should help fight poverty and discrimination around the world not out of charity, or at least not solely out of charity, but because it is in their own self-interest to do so.

Of course, discrimination, poverty, and population growth may not be independent. In particular, population growth may contribute to poverty. If this is so, the case for limiting population growth as a means of promoting the future availability of mineral commodities is easier to make. If population growth does not aggravate poverty, however, it is far less clear that mineral commodity availability is a valid justification for curbing population growth.

Living on Borrowed Time?

So are we living on borrowed time? Is modern civilization as we know it threatened by the depletion of oil and other mineral commodities? Are drastic public policies needed to avert disaster and to provide a secure future for generations to come? Are public policies needed simply as a precaution or as insurance against the possibility that depletion may be a problem in the future?

Modern-day prophets cry out yes, and yes again, to all of these questions. They call upon society to repent and to mend its ways. To curb its population growth. To restrain its use of mineral resources. To tame its passion for more and better things. To turn away from materialism, and to embrace a simpler life.

Standing at the other end of the spectrum are the prophet slayers. They claim the availability of mineral resources poses no problems, now and forevermore (or at least for as long as we might have an interest in the future). They contend that our prophets are not prophets at all, but Chicken Littles running about crying that the sky is falling.

The public is fascinated with its prophets and prophet slayers. They come with clear and uncomplicated messages, painting the world in black and white. They tell us what we need to know, what we need to think, and what we should or should not do. They are colorful, passionate, and so convinced they are right that it is hard to resist being swept up in their enthusiasm.

The real world, however, is not so simple. Rarely is it painted in black and white. Rather, it is bedecked in hues of gray and in a palette of bright colors. It is full of risks, uncertainties, unknowns, and complications—all traits that make life interesting, exciting, and challenging, even if at times frustrating and troubling as well.

And so it is with our fears of mineral depletion. During the next 50 to 100 years, we have found that mineral depletion is not likely to rank among the most pressing problems confronting society. The great beyond, however, depends on the race between the cost-increasing effects of depletion and the cost-reducing effects of new technology. The outcome will be influenced by many factors, and is simply unknown. Although more geologic information about the nature and incidence of uneconomic mineral deposits would provide useful insights, even this would not completely eliminate the uncertainty.

What, then, is the appropriate role for public policy? Falling back on the precautionary principle, some contend that society should restrict the use of primary mineral resources by constraining population growth, by slowing economic growth, and by promoting recycling, conservation, and the greater use of renewable resources. We have seen, however, that such policies are not risk free, and can be counterproductive. Even if this is not the case, cheaper ways to buy the same or more protection may exist. These concerns do not necessarily mean that all public policies in these areas are undesirable, but they do sound a cautionary note. Such initiatives, they warn, need to be carefully scrutinized.

A far clearer case exists for policies that internalize the environmental and other social costs incurred in the production and use of mineral commodities.

Over time, environmental costs are accounting for a rising share of the total costs of producing and using mineral commodities. Good public policies that force producers and consumers to pay these costs can favorably influence the race between depletion and technology by providing producers and users with strong incentives to reduce these costs. Such policies are in any case desirable for other reasons.

Internalizing the full social costs of mineral production and use, however, will not be easy. A major challenge is the development of reliable and acceptable tools for measuring external costs, particularly in light of the great differences among people in the values that they attach to indigenous cultures, biodiversity, stable global climate, and other environmental assets. Although the past several decades have seen much progress in this area, more is needed. Also of importance is the strengthening of the institutions and political resolve to provide governments with the will and the means to internalize social costs once they are adequately identified and measured. As global warming and artisanal mining so clearly illustrate, this can be difficult.

A strong case can also be made for public policies that encourage the development of the new technologies to offset the cost-increasing effects of depletion. Such technology is the major weapon in the arsenal that society has at its disposal for keeping the threat of mineral depletion at bay. Because many of the benefits flowing from new technology cannot be fully captured by the firms and other organizations responsible for its generation, public support is needed to ensure that sufficient funding is available for this effort. This, of course, is true not just for research and development on mineral production and use, but more generally for most research and development. And, of course, many governments do support research and development in the mineral sector and other fields.

Whether more public funding is desirable for new technologies in the mineral sector is an important issue that deserves more attention. Many scientists and engineers who have devoted their professional lives to geology, mining and petroleum engineering, metallurgy, and other related fields claim many new technologies lie on the horizon that will pay very handsome dividends to society if only the necessary investment in research and development is undertaken.[6]

In an important sense, we are living on borrowed time. The world is in transition. Although this is not new, and indeed has been true since the earth was created, what is new is the pace of change. A century ago, we relied heavily upon wood and coal to heat our homes and drive the economy. Today, we use much more oil, natural gas, and nuclear power. A century from now, the mix will certainly be different again. Those who claim that our reliance on conventional oil and rich mineral deposits—copper deposits blessed with grades of 0.8 percent and higher—must decline are probably right. But this is not particularly interesting, or relevant, for sustainable development and the welfare of future generations.

The important question is whether society will be able in the future to provide the needs currently being served by these high-quality mineral deposits from other resources at real prices close to or even below those that currently prevail. Nonrenewable mineral resources make it abundantly clear that the world without change, even if it were desirable, is simply not sustainable. The current exploitation of high-quality mineral resources provides society with the opportunity to develop the new technologies that will allow it to satisfy its future needs from other resources without despoiling its environment or destroying other important social assets.

Although Mother Nature may define the nature of the challenge—the rules of the game, if you wish—she has been quite generous. So humankind will largely determine whether or not the outcome is favorable. If we fail to meet the challenge, the threat of mineral exhaustion will grow more serious, and scarcity could ultimately impose a significant constraint on economic development and the welfare of future generations. If we rise to the challenge, the threat of mineral exhaustion will recede and mineral commodities will become more and more available. The future, in short, is there for us to seize and shape.

Notes

1. For this and other reasons, there are no very long-run future markets for mineral commodities, where one might, for example, buy oil for delivery 50 or 100 years in the future. The absence of such markets may introduce some myopia in assessing scarcity, as observers focus on the present and very near future where market prices do exist.

2. This presumes that solar sites are readily available and of similar quality, both in terms of the availability of incoming solar power and in terms of location to markets. Because this is not the case, Ricardian rent and possibly user costs as well might arise in practice. They would be reflected in the land prices for solar collection sites.

3. The same rationale can be employed to justify government support for research and development that reduces the cost of recycling and so promotes secondary production. Here, however, the argument of market failure supports government funding for research and development that also reduces the costs of primary production. So whether optimal public support for research and development would favor secondary or primary production is unclear.

4. See Ackerman 1997 for a recent and well-developed example of this position.

5. Kolstad (1996) makes a similar, though more sophisticated, argument for proceeding more slowly on global warming policies. With respect both to recycling and to global warming, one might contend that it will be too late for policy to be helpful if one waits until the problem is clear. Why this should be so in the case of recycling, though, is far from clear.

6. As I was writing these lines, the National Research Council announced the completion of a study by a panel of scientists examining the results of the $13 billion that the U.S. Department of Energy has spent since 1978 on more efficient ways of using energy and of burning fossil fuels. The study (National Research Council 2001) found that the $13 billion investment generated about $40 billion in economic benefits. It is interesting that almost three-quarters of the benefits came from three research programs, which together cost just $11 million. Research, it appears, is like exploration. A few highly successful projects more than compensate for the many less successful efforts.

For another recent study of relevance, one with which I was associated, see National Research Council 2002. This investigation focuses largely on the nonfuel minerals, and also concludes that the benefits to society of additional research and development on ways to find and produce mineral commodities far exceed the costs.

References

Ackerman, F. 1997. *Why Do We Recycle? Markets, Values, and Public Policy*. Washington, DC: Island Press.

Daly, H. 1996. *Beyond Growth: The Economics of Sustainable Development*. Boston: Beacon Press.

Dasgupta, P., and G. Heal. 1979. *Economic Theory and Exhaustible Resources*. Cambridge: Cambridge University Press.

Dasgupta, P., and others. 1999. Intergenerational Equity, Social Discount Rates, and Global Warming. In *Discounting and Intergenerational Equity*, edited by P.R. Portney and J.P. Weyant. Washington, DC: Resources for the Future.

Hartwick, J.M. 1977. Intergenerational Equity and the Investing of Rents from Exhaustible Resources. *American Economic Review* 67: 972–974.

Kolstad, C.D. 1996. Learning and Stock Effects in Environmental Regulation: The Case of Greenhouse Gas Emissions. *Journal of Environmental Economics and Management* 31: 1–18.

Krutilla, J.V., and A.C. Fisher. 1975. *The Economics of Natural Environments: Studies in the Valuation of Commodity and Amenity Resources*. Baltimore, MD: Johns Hopkins University Press for Resources for the Future.

National Research Council, Board on Energy and Environment Systems. 2001a. *Energy Research at DOE: Was It Worth It?* Washington, DC: National Academy Press.

National Research Council, Board on Earth Sciences and Resources. 2001b. *Evolutionary and Revolutionary Technologies for Mining*. Washington, DC: National Academy Press.

Neumayer, E. 2000. Scarce or Abundant? The Economics of Natural Resource Availability. *Journal of Economic Surveys* 14(3): 307–335.

Nordhaus, W.D., and E.C. Kokkelenberg (eds.). 1999. *Nature's Numbers: Expanding the National Economic Accounts to Include the Environment*. Washington, DC: National Academy Press for the National Research Council.

Page, T. 1977. *Conservation and Economic Efficiency: An Approach to Materials Policy*. Baltimore, MD: Johns Hopkins University Press for Resources for the Future.

Ruth, M. 1995. Thermodynamic Implications for Natural Resource Extraction and Technical Change in U.S. Copper Mining. *Environmental and Resource Economics* 6(2): 187–206.

Simon, J.L. 1981. *The Ultimate Resource*. Princeton, NJ: Princeton University Press.

———. 1990. *Population Matters: People, Resources, Environment, and Immigration*. New Brunswick, NJ: Transactions Press.

Solow, R.M. 1974. Intergenerational Equity and Exhaustible Resources. *Review of Economic Studies, Symposium on the Economics of Exhaustible Resources*: 29–45.

Toman, M.A. 1992. The Difficulty in Defining Sustainability. In *Global Development and the Environment: Perspectives on Sustainability*, edited by J. Darmstadter. Washington, DC: Resources for the Future.

World Bank. 2001. *World Development Report 2000/2001*. www.worldbank.org.

World Commission on Environment and Development. 1987. *Our Common Future*. Oxford: Oxford University Press.

Appendix:
Real Prices for Selected Mineral Commodities, 1870–1997

by Peter Howie

The figures below show the prices for aluminum, copper, pig iron, iron ore, nickel, lead, silver, tin, zinc, petroleum, natural gas, and bituminous coal deflated by the U.S. producer price index over the period 1870 to 1997. They are an update of the price data that Robert S. Manthy provides in his 1978 book, *Natural Resource Commodities—A Century of Statistics*. This book, in turn, updates the 1962 book by Neal Potter and Francis T. Christy, Jr., *Trends in Natural Resource Commodities*. Both volumes, published by Johns Hopkins University Press for Resources for the Future, contain a wealth of other data on mineral output, consumption, trade, and employment.

It is important to note that the prices shown are for the United States. Many mineral commodities are sold in global markets, and so trends in U.S. prices closely track prices abroad. However, this is not always the case. For example, the iron ore price shown is for iron ore from the Mesabi Range in northern Minnesota sold at ports on Lake Erie. This price does not fully reflect the decline during the past several decades in the prices of iron ore shipped from Brazil and Australia, which are currently the world's largest producers and exporters of iron ore.

The data sources for the following figures identify the nature of the prices quoted along with their original sources.

Peter Howie is a visiting assistant professor in the Department of Economics at the University of Montana.

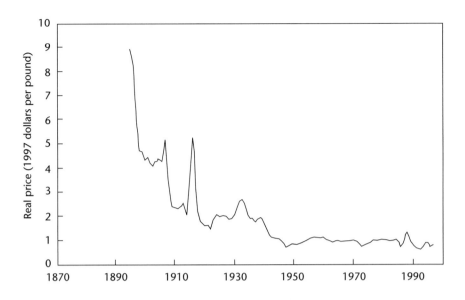

Aluminum—New York Prices and Producers' Average Price for Ingot, 1895–1997

Sources:

1895 to 1957 data from N. Potter and F.T. Christy, Jr., *Trends in Natural Resource Commodities: Statistics of Prices, Output, Consumption, Foreign Trade, and Employment in the United States, 1870–1957* (Baltimore, MD: Johns Hopkins University Press for Resources for the Future, 1962).

1958 to 1983 data from the annual publication *Metal Statistics* (New York: American Metal Market).

1984 to 1991 data from the *ABMS Non-Ferrous Metals Data Yearbook* (Chatham, NJ: American Bureau of Metal Statistics).

1992 to 1997 data from the annual publication *Metal Statistics* (New York: American Metal Market).

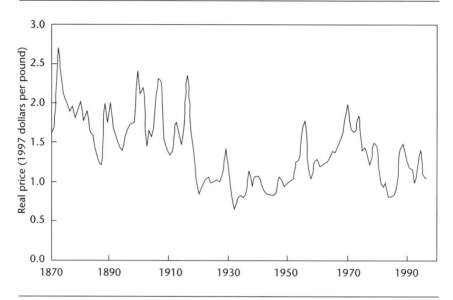

Copper—U.S. Ingot and Electrolytic Copper Prices at Refinery, 1870–1997

Sources:

1870 to 1957 data from N. Potter and F.T. Christy, Jr., *Trends in Natural Resource Commodities: Statistics of Prices, Output, Consumption, Foreign Trade, and Employment in the United States, 1870–1957* (Baltimore, MD: Johns Hopkins University Press for Resources for the Future, 1962).

1958 to 1973 data from R.S. Manthey, *Natural Resource Commodities—A Century of Statistics: Prices, Output, Consumption, Foreign Trade, and Employment in the United States, 1870–1973* (Baltimore, MD: Johns Hopkins University Press for Resources for the Future, 1978).

1974 to 1997 data from the *ABMS Non-Ferrous Metals Data Yearbook* (Chatham, NJ: American Bureau of Metal Statistics).

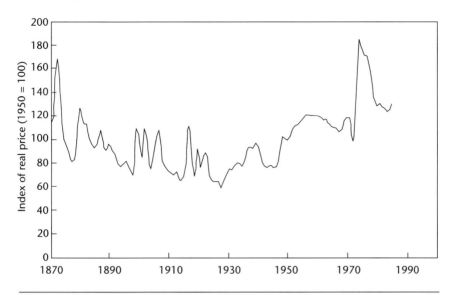

Pig Iron—U.S. Average Value, 1870–1986

Sources:

1870 to 1957 data from N. Potter and F.T. Christy, Jr., *Trends in Natural Resource Commodities: Statistics of Prices, Output, Consumption, Foreign Trade, and Employment in the United States, 1870–1957* (Baltimore, MD: Johns Hopkins University Press for Resources for the Future, 1962).

1958 to 1973 data from R.S. Manthey, *Natural Resource Commodities—A Century of Statistics: Prices, Output, Consumption, Foreign Trade, and Employment in the United States, 1870–1973* (Baltimore, MD: Johns Hopkins University Press for Resources for the Future, 1978).

1974 to 1986 data from the Bureau of Labor Statistics's monthly periodical, *Wholesale Prices and Price Indexes*.

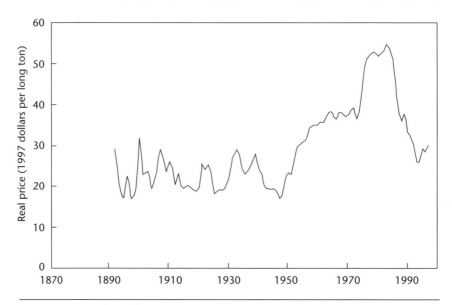

Iron Ore—Price of Mesabi, Non-Bessemer Iron Ore at Lake Erie Docks, 1895–1997

Sources:

1895 to 1957 data from N. Potter and F.T. Christy, Jr., *Trends in Natural Resource Commodities: Statistics of Prices, Output, Consumption, Foreign Trade, and Employment in the United States, 1870–1957* (Baltimore, MD: Johns Hopkins University Press for Resources for the Future, 1962).

1958 to 1997 data from the Salient Iron Ore Statistics (average value at mines) in the U.S. Geological Survey's *Mineral Yearbook* (Washington, DC: U.S. Government Printing Office).

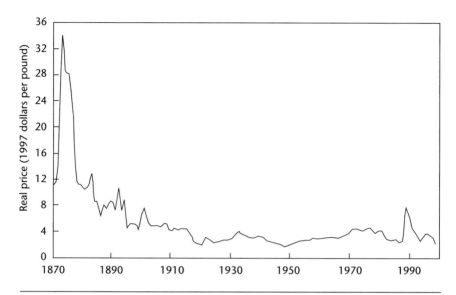

Nickel—Average Unit Value Imported for Consumption, 1870–1997

Sources:

1870 to 1957 data from N. Potter and F.T. Christy, Jr., *Trends in Natural Resource Commodities: Statistics of Prices, Output, Consumption, Foreign Trade, and Employment in the United States, 1870–1957* (Baltimore, MD: Johns Hopkins University Press for Resources for the Future, 1962).

1958 to1990 data from the U.S. Geological Survey's 1993 *Statistical Compendium* at h (accessed September 23, 2002).

1991 to 1997 data from the U.S. Geological Survey's *Mineral Yearbook* (Washington, DC: U.S. Government Printing Office).

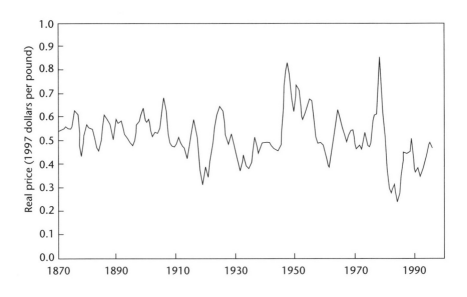

Lead—U.S. Average Price in New York, 1870–1997

Sources:

1870 to 1957 data from N. Potter and F.T. Christy, Jr., *Trends in Natural Resource Commodities: Statistics of Prices, Output, Consumption, Foreign Trade, and Employment in the United States, 1870–1957* (Baltimore, MD: Johns Hopkins University Press for Resources for the Future, 1962).

1958 to 1973 data from R.S. Manthey, *Natural Resource Commodities—A Century of Statistics: Prices, Output, Consumption, Foreign Trade, and Employment in the United States, 1870–1973* (Baltimore, MD: Johns Hopkins University Press for Resources for the Future, 1978).

1974 to 1987 data from the U.S. producer lead price in the *ABMS Non-Ferrous Metals Data Yearbook* (Chatham, NJ: American Bureau of Metal Statistics).

1988 to 1997 data from the North American producer lead price in the *ABMS Non-Ferrous Metals Data Yearbook* (Chatham, NJ: American Bureau of Metal Statistics).

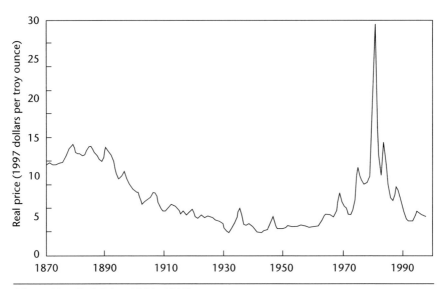

Silver—New York Price, 1870–1997

Sources:

1870 to 1957 data from the U.S. Bureau of the Census, *Historical Statistics of the United States, Colonial Times to 1957* (Washington, DC: U.S. Government Printing Office, 1960).

1958 to 1997 data from the annual publication *Metal Statistics* (New York: American Metal Market).

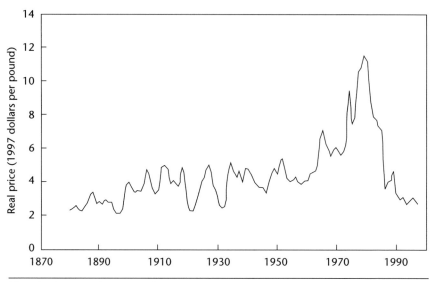

Tin—Straits Prices in New York, 1880–1997

Source:

1880 to 1997 data from the annual publication *Metal Statistics* (New York: American Metal Market).

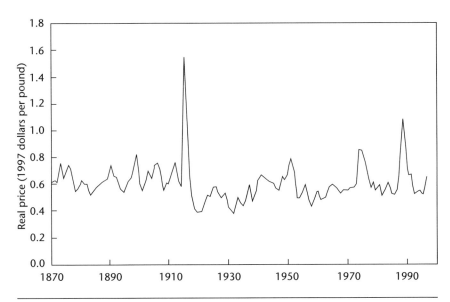

Zinc—Prime Western Slab Delivered in the United States, 1870–1997

Sources:

1870 to 1957 data from N. Potter and F.T. Christy, Jr., *Trends in Natural Resource Commodities: Statistics of Prices, Output, Consumption, Foreign Trade, and Employment in the United States, 1870–1957* (Baltimore, MD: Johns Hopkins University Press for Resources for the Future, 1962).

1958 to 1973 data from R.S. Manthey, *Natural Resource Commodities—A Century of Statistics: Prices, Output, Consumption, Foreign Trade, and Employment in the United States, 1870–1973* (Baltimore, MD: Johns Hopkins University Press for Resources for the Future, 1978).

1974 to 1990 data from the annual publication *Metal Statistics* (New York: American Metal Market).

1991 data is based on an average of London Metals Exchange quotes.

1992 to 1997 data from the producers U.S. spot zinc and prime Western Slab zinc in the annual publication *Metal Statistics* (New York: American Metal Market).

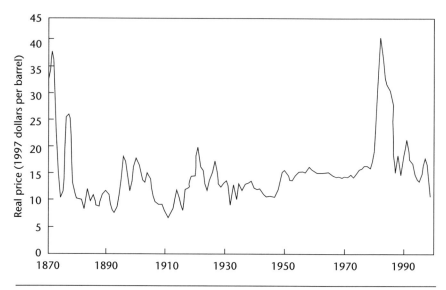

Petroleum—U.S. Average Value, 1870–1997

Sources:

1870 to 1957 data from N. Potter and F.T. Christy, Jr., *Trends in Natural Resource Commodities: Statistics of Prices, Output, Consumption, Foreign Trade, and Employment in the United States, 1870–1957* (Baltimore, MD: Johns Hopkins University Press for Resources for the Future, 1962).

1958 to 1973 data from R.S. Manthey, *Natural Resource Commodities—A Century of Statistics: Prices, Output, Consumption, Foreign Trade, and Employment in the United States, 1870–1973* (Baltimore, MD: Johns Hopkins University Press for Resources for the Future, 1978).

1974 to 1997 data from the semiannual publication *Basic Petroleum Data Book* (Washington, DC: American Petroleum Institute).

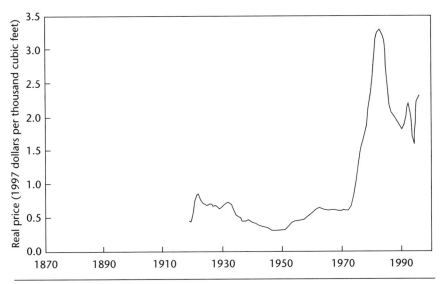

Natural Gas—U.S. Average Value, Point of Production, 1919–1997

Sources:

1919 to 1957 data from N. Potter and F.T. Christy, Jr., *Trends in Natural Resource Commodities: Statistics of Prices, Output, Consumption, Foreign Trade, and Employment in the United States, 1870–1957* (Baltimore, MD: Johns Hopkins University Press for Resources for the Future, 1962).

1958 to 1973 data from R.S. Manthey, *Natural Resource Commodities—A Century of Statistics: Prices, Output, Consumption, Foreign Trade, and Employment in the United States, 1870–1973* (Baltimore, MD: Johns Hopkins University Press for Resources for the Future, 1978).

1974 to 1997 data from the *Historical Natural Gas Annual* (Washington, DC: American Petroleum Institute).

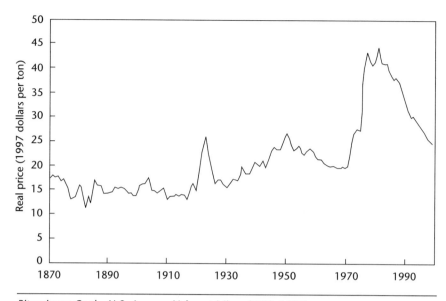

Bituminous Coal—U.S. Average Value at Mine, 1870–1997

Sources:

1870 to 1957 data from N. Potter and F.T. Christy, Jr., *Trends in Natural Resource Commodities: Statistics of Prices, Output, Consumption, Foreign Trade, and Employment in the United States, 1870–1957* (Baltimore, MD: Johns Hopkins University Press for Resources for the Future, 1962).

1958 to 1973 data from R.S. Manthey, *Natural Resource Commodities—A Century of Statistics: Prices, Output, Consumption, Foreign Trade, and Employment in the United States, 1870–1973* (Baltimore, MD: Johns Hopkins University Press for Resources for the Future, 1978).

1974 to 1997 data from the Energy Information Administration, *Annual Energy Review* (Washington, DC: U.S. Government Printing Office).

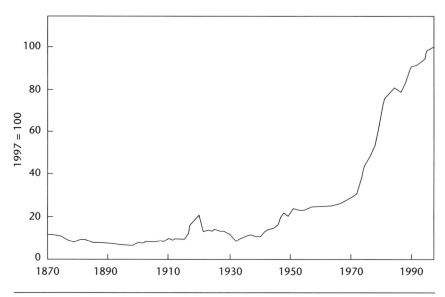

All Commodities—Producer Price Index, 1870–1997

Sources:

1870 to 1957 data from N. Potter and F.T. Christy, Jr., *Trends in Natural Resource Commodities: Statistics of Prices, Output, Consumption, Foreign Trade, and Employment in the United States, 1870–1957* (Baltimore, MD: Johns Hopkins University Press for Resources for the Future, 1962).

1958 to 1973 data from R.S. Manthey, *Natural Resource Commodities—A Century of Statistics: Prices, Output, Consumption, Foreign Trade, and Employment in the United States, 1870–1973* (Baltimore, MD: Johns Hopkins University Press for Resources for the Future, 1978).

1974 to 1997 data from the annual U.S. Bureau of the Census publication *Statistical Abstracts of the United States* (Washington, DC: U.S. Government Printing Office).

Glossary

Artisanal mining: Mining on a very small scale using simple and unmechanized equipment. It often is illegal, and tends to be inefficient, dangerous, and highly polluting. See Chapter 6 and Box 6-3.

Availability: The sacrifice in terms of a representative basket of goods and services that must be forgone to obtain an additional unit of a commodity. When the basket of goods and services is growing, the commodity is becoming less available or more scarce. When one commodity requires a bigger basket than another, it is less available or more scarce. See Chapter 1.

Average cost: The total cost of production for a good divided by the number of units produced.

Cash costs: In the mining industry, cash costs are production costs minus capital costs (specifically, depreciation, amortization, and interest on external debt). Cash costs approximate what economists call variable costs, which are costs that increase or decrease with output (e.g., labor and energy costs).

Command-and-control regulations: Government requirements designed to improve the environment or for other purposes that prescribe how firms should operate. See Chapter 6.

Contingent valuation: A technique for valuing environmental and other nonmarket goods that involves asking people what they would be willing to pay to preserve such goods. See Chapter 6.

Cumulative supply: A curve that shows how much producers of a mineral commodity, such as copper or oil, will supply over all time at various prices assuming that technology and all other determinants of supply other than price remain fixed at certain specified levels. It applies only to nonrenewable resources, and it differs from the traditional supply curve. The latter shows how much producers of a good will supply at various prices during a year or some other time period.

Demand curve: A line that shows how much the users of a commodity will demand as its price varies, assuming that all other determinants of demand, such as the price of substitutes, remain fixed at some specific level.

Depletion: The use of high-quality, low-cost mineral deposits that requires society over time to exploit lower-quality deposits.

Disturbance term: A variable included in equations in econometric models that takes account of the influence of omitted variables, measurement errors, and other factors that cause the actual value of the dependent variable to vary from what the estimated equation anticipates. See Chapter 4.

Econometric model: One or more equations derived on the basis of economic reasoning whose unknown parameters are estimated by various statistical techniques. See Chapter 4.

Economic rent: See *rent.*

Existence value: See *nonuse value.*

External benefits: Benefits associated with the production and use of a good or some other activity that are not captured by producers and consumers. An example might be research and development activities by a mining company on mine site restoration that produces useful information for other mining companies as well. See Chapter 6.

External costs: Costs associated with the production and use of a good or some other activity that are not paid for by producers and consumers, and so are borne by third parties. An example might be the pollution of a river by a mining operation, the costs of which are borne by those who use the river below the mine. See Chapter 6.

Externalities: External costs, external benefits, or both. See Chapter 6.

Fixed-stock paradigm: A view of mineral depletion that assumes that the supply of any mineral commodity is a fixed or given quantity (a fixed stock). Depletion occurs as demand, which is a flow variable continuing year after year, consumes the available supply. See Chapters 5 and 7.

Fuels: Mineral commodities, such as oil, natural gas, coal, and uranium, that are valued for their ability to produce useful energy. See Chapter 1 and Box 1-1.

Green accounting: National income and product accounts that take into consideration the availability and use of the environment and other natural resources. See Chapter 7.

Hotelling rent: See *user cost.*

Inflation adjustment: Removing from the price trend for a particular good or service the average trend in price for all commodities (inflation). Deflators, such as the producer price index, the gross domestic product (GDP) deflator, and the consumer price index, are used for this purpose.

Intensity of use: The quantity of a mineral commodity consumed, normally measured in tons, barrels, or other physical units, divided by gross domestic product or other measures of income, normally measured in real dollars. See Chapter 5.

Internalized costs: Costs of producing and using a good that the producers and in turn the consumers pay for. In contrast to external costs, internalized costs, which are also called private costs, are not borne by third parties. See Chapter 6.

Long run: Traditionally, the long run (or long term) in economics is several years or more, a period that is sufficient for the building of new capacity or the retirement of unneeded capacity. In this study, the long run is occasionally used in this sense. More frequently, however, it refers to a period of 50 years or more.

Marginal benefit: The benefit from producing one more unit of a good.

Marginal cost: The cost of producing one more unit of a good.

McKelvey box: A two-dimensional figure proposed by the geologist Vincent McKelvey, which distinguishes between resources and reserves on the basis of economic and geological conditions. See Chapter 3.

Metals and metal alloys: A subset of mineral commodities used primarily as materials. Metals such as copper, lead, zinc, iron, and aluminum are elements. They are for the most part solid at ordinary temperatures, opaque, and good conductors of electricity and heat. Alloys are a combination of two or more metals or of a metal and certain nonmetals such as carbon. Bronze, for example, is an alloy of copper and tin. Steel is an alloy of iron, carbon, and possibly other metals as well. See Chapter 1 and Box 1-1.

Mineral commodities: The end products (fuels, metals, and nonmetals) produced from mineral resources and from the recycling of scrap. See Chapter 1 and Box 1-1.

Mineral depletion: See *depletion.*

Mineral resources: The subsurface deposits from which metals, fuels, and other mineral commodities are produced. See Chapter 1.

Nominal costs and prices: Costs and prices (in U.S. dollars or another currency) that have not been adjusted for inflation. See Chapter 3 and Box 3-4.

Nonmetals: Mineral commodities that are not fuels, metals, or metal alloys. They include limestone, sand and gravel, phosphate rock, and sulfur. They are used primarily for construction, industrial applications, and fertilizer production. See Chapter 1 and Box 1-1.

Nonrenewable resources: Resources, such as oil fields and copper deposits, that require millions of years to form, and so cannot be replenished on a time scale of relevance to humanity. See Chapters 1 and 7.

Nonuse value: The value that individuals derive from certain resources (e.g., pristine wilderness) even though they will never use them directly (e.g., visit the wilderness). Other terms used to indicate nonuse value include existence value, passive use value, preservation value, bequest value, stewardship value, and intrinsic value. See Chapter 6.

Opportunity cost: The value of what must be sacrificed to obtain a good. For example, the opportunity cost for a cleaner environment may be somewhat higher prices for mineral commodities. See Chapter 1.

Opportunity-cost paradigm: A view of mineral depletion that relies upon what society must sacrifice in terms of other goods and services (the opportunity costs) to obtain more of a mineral commodity. When the real price of oil is falling, for example, society must give up less of other goods and services to get an additional barrel over time. This, according to the opportunity-cost paradigm, means that oil is becoming more available or less scarce. See Chapters 5 and 7.

Parameter: An unknown constant in the equation or equations of an econometric model that can be estimated by various statistical techniques. See Chapter 4.

Pigovian tax: A fee imposed per unit of pollution that is set equal to the damage that an additional or marginal unit of pollution imposes on the environment. It thus forces firms and other polluters to pay the full social costs of their pollution. Named after Arthur Pigou, the British economist.

Present value: The value today of revenues to be received or costs to be paid in the future. Because the time value of money is positive, in part because money can be invested and earn interest, a dollar today is worth more than a dollar a year from now. Present-value techniques adjust funds to be received or paid in the future for the time value of money, and thereby indicate the value of these obligations today. See Chapter 2 and Box 2-1.

Primary production: The output of mineral commodities from subsurface mineral deposits. See Chapter 3 and Box 3-1.

Private costs: See *internalized costs.*

Public goods: Goods, such as national defense, which if provided are available for all to consume. See Chapter 6.

Real costs and prices: Costs and prices in U.S. dollars or another currency that have been adjusted for inflation. See Chapter 3 and Box 3-4.

Renewable resources: Resources, such as timber and fish, that can be replenished within a relatively short period of time (within years or decades). See Chapters 1 and 7.

Rent: Any payment to the owner of a factor of production (labor, land, mineral resources) above that necessary for the owner to offer the factor in the marketplace. For a factor of production already offered in the marketplace, rent is any payment above that necessary to keep the factor in the marketplace. See Chapters 2 and 3 and Box 3-5. Also see *Ricardian rent.*

Reserves: All of a mineral commodity contained in deposits that are known and economic to exploit under current conditions (prices, technology). See Chapter 3 and Figure 3-1.

Resource base: All of a mineral commodity contained in the earth's crust. The reserve base for a mineral commodity encompasses its resources and its reserves. See Chapter 3 and Figure 3-1.

Resources: All of a mineral commodity contained in deposits (1) that are currently known or expected to be discovered under prescribed conditions and (2) that are currently economic to exploit or are expected to be economic to exploit under prescribed conditions. See Chapter 3 and Figure 3-1.

Ricardian rent: Payment to the owners of land or mineral deposits above that necessary to entice the owners to offer their land or deposits to the marketplace. Ricardian rent arises because much land and many mineral deposits are of higher quality (and hence have lower costs) than the poorest-quality land or deposits required to satisfy existing demand. See Chapters 2 and 3 and Box 3-5.

Scarcity: A shortage or lack of availability. Rising real prices for a commodity, for example, are an indication of growing scarcity. See Chapter 1.

Scarcity rent: See *user costs.*

Secondary production: The production of mineral commodities, primarily metals, from the recycling of scrap. See Chapter 3 and Box 3-1.

Short run: Any period of time that is less than the long run.

Shortage: An excess of demand over the available supply at the prevailing market price, or the balancing of supply and demand by a rising market price that leaves many traditional consumers unable to afford the commodity. A growing shortage implies increasing scarcity and declining availability. See Chapter 1.

Small-scale mining: Artisanal mining plus mining on a slightly larger scale including modest operations with some mechanized equipment. See Chapter 6 and Box 6-3.

Social cost: The full cost to society of producing and using a good, which includes the internalized or private costs (those borne by the producers and consumers) as well as any external costs (those borne by third parties).

Social welfare: See *welfare.*

Stationary trend: A series of data over time that reverts back to the same long-run trend if disturbed by a short-term shock. See Chapter 4.

Stochastic trend: A series of data over time that does not revert back to the same long-run trend if disturbed by a short-term shock. See Chapter 4.

Supply curve: A line that shows how much the producers of a commodity will supply during a year or some other period of time as its price varies, assuming that all other determinants of supply, such as the costs of labor, remain fixed at some specific level. See Chapter 5.

Sustainability: See *sustainable development.*

Sustainable development: Behavior that does not preclude future generations from enjoying a standard of living comparable to that of today. See Chapter 7.

System dynamics: A method for studying and understanding how complex systems, such as the global economy, change over time. Internal feedback loops within the structure of the system govern the behavior of the entire system.

User costs: The present value of the lost future profits caused by producing one more unit of a mineral commodity today. The decline in future profits arises because increased production today leaves less or poorer-quality mineral deposits in the ground for future exploitation. User costs are also called Hotelling rent and scarcity rent. See Chapters 2 and 3 and Box 3-5.

Welfare: The condition or well-being of society as measured by per capita real income or other indicators (e.g., infant mortality, educational levels, income distribution, and longevity).

Index

In page references, n. indicates an endnote, and italicized letters indicate boxes *(b)*, figures *(f)*, or tables *(t)*.

Accounting, green. *See* Green accounting
Acid Rain Program, 87
Agriculture
  evolution of availability concerns, 7–8, 11, 16(n.1)
  production cost trends, 37, 38*t*
  real price trends, 39, 40*f*, 41
Alcoa, 89
Aluminum
  plastic substitution, 73
  production cost trends, 38
  real price trends, 41, 45, 125*f*
  recycling, 74
  reserve life expectancies, 21*t*
  resource base life expectancies, 23*t*
  social cost issues, 89, 91*f*, 98(n.4)
Amazon region social cost issues, 85–86*b*
Anthropocentric marketplace focus, 32–33

Arsenic emissions, 89, 91*f*
Artisinal mining, 5, 96, 97*b*
Asbestos, 53
Asset accounts, 106–7
Asteroid mining, 24
Atomic substitution, 66–67*b*
Australia, Coronation Hill Project, 94*b*
Automobiles
  alternative fuels, 24
  policy issues, 33
  recycling scrap, 20*b*
  social cost issues, 83
  technological advances, 74
Availability. *See* Mineral resource availability
Average costs, 29. *See also* Mineral production costs

Barnett and Morse (1963), 10–11, 37–42, 48–49, 55(n.4)
Benefits of environmental resource use. *See* Marginal benefits; Marginal net benefit curves
Beyond the Limits. See Meadows and others (1992)
Biodiversity
  evolution of availability concerns, 12

social cost issues, 87, 92–93, 98(n.2)
Uranium, 2*b*
U.S. Export Unit Values index, 49*f*
U.S. Geological Survey, 19
Use of minerals. *See* Mineral
    consumption
User costs. *See also* Opportunity costs
    definition of, 50
    economic measures overview, 26–31,
        34(n.3), 53, 102
    exhaustible resources theory, 14
    findings and implications, 111
    green accounting, 107–8, 121(n.2)
    historical trends, 36, 50–53, 56(nn.13,
        14)
    real price trends and, 42–43, 44*f*, 45,
        50–53
    use of term, 28
U-shaped curve hypotheses
    intensity of use, 72–73
    mineral commodity prices, 29, 42–43,
        54

Value, present. *See* Present value concept
Valuing environmental and social
    goods, 92–95, 98, 99(nn.7, 8), 103,
    120

Wages, 37, 53, 55(n.5)

Wealth. *See* Income distribution issues
Welfare. *See also* Social costs
    evolution of availability concerns,
        7–8
    findings and implications, 104–5,
        107, 109, 112, 118, 120
    forecasting issues, 63
    market flaws, 32
    terminology, 4
Wilderness
    findings and implications, 108–9
    social cost issues, 92–94, 99(n.6)
Workers. *See* Labor
World income. *See* Income, per capita;
        Income distribution issues
World population. *See* Population
World reserves. *See also* Reserves
    forecasting issues, 60
    life expectancies of, 19, 21*t*
World War I, 47
World War II, 10

Zinc
    forecasting issues, 66*b*
    real price trends, 41, 45, 55(n.10),
        133*f*
    reserve life expectancies, 19, 21*t*
    resource base life expectancies, 23*t*, 24

About the Author

John E. Tilton is the William J. Coulter Professor of Mineral Economics in the Division of Economics and Business at the Colorado School of Mines and a university fellow at Resources for the Future. His teaching and research interests over the past 30 years have focused on economic and policy issues associated with mining and the metal industries. His most recent work examines the environment and mining, material substitution, long-run trends in metal demand, the recycling of metals, the sources of productivity growth in mining, and changes in comparative advantage in metal trade.

In 1977, Professor Tilton served as an economics affairs officer for the Mineral and Metals Branch of the United Nations Conference on Trade and Development in Switzerland. From 1982 to 1984, he directed a research program on mineral trade and markets at the International Institute for Applied Systems Analysis in Austria. More recently, he has been a visiting fellow at Resources for the Future, a senior Fulbright scholar at the École Nationale Supérieure des Mines in Paris and a visiting scholar at the Centro de Minería at the Pontificia Universidad Católica de Chile in Santiago. He has also served on various boards and committees of the National Research Council, including most recently the Panel on Integrated Environmental and Economic Accounting and the Committee to Study Technologies for the Mining Industries.

In recognition for his contributions in the field of mineral economics, he has received the Mineral Economics Award from the Society for Mining, Metallurgy, and Exploration, the Distinguished Service Award from the Mineral Economics and Management Society, the N.M. Rothschild Visiting Professorship in Mineral Economics from Curtin University in Australia, and an honorary doctorate from the Lulea University of Technology in Sweden.